I Was Just Leaving

I Was Just Leaving

Reflections on Growing Old

Mary Cushman

ISBN-13: 979-8-218-12238-6

Cover Design: Lori Harley
Author Photo: Lee Bowman

In loving memory of my father,
who never got a chance to grow old

Oh, as I was young and easy in the mercy of his means
Time held me green and dying
Though I sang in my chains like the sea.

—DYLAN THOMAS,
from *"Fern Hill"*

Contents

Introductory Note

In old age, a feeling grows that you are on the verge of being launched. It's a sense that you are almost done *here*, and you are about to be *there*. None of us knows, of course, where "there" is, but we know for sure it's not here. This feeling accounts for the title of the book. It isn't about being unwelcome, as the phrase usually implies. Instead, it names an awareness of being called forward, called elsewhere...even as we continue to look back at our disappearing tracks.

Facing Into the Wind

My delaying tactics are evident everywhere. They're in the jumble of old shoes on the floor of my bedroom closet. They're part of the leavings in my bottom bureau drawer: the almost-new panty hose, gift scarves I've never worn, a battered jewelry box holding useless single earrings. And that same delay long ago settled onto my mother's cups and saucers, stashed for years in the back of our kitchen cupboard.

All my timeworn items may seem like clutter to be discarded lickety-split. But once we've passed into our seventies—and I'm well in at seventy-nine—meaning can collect on orphaned earrings and old saucers. These remnants of a life carry an undeniable message: the day is soon coming when my need for *any* closets or cupboards or bureau drawers will be moot.

No matter how many more years I may actually live, such items contain a reminder that while it might be prudent to tidy up, timelier challenges press in on my husband Tom and me. Like writing our obituaries. Designing and ordering a tombstone. Choosing a shrub for the cemetery plot on the island in Maine where we live. Picking music and readings to include in our funeral services.

Focus on these matters, even when we are older, is often viewed as morbid. But some of the people I have admired most seem able to deal decisively with life's inevitable clutter, and embrace these more daunting tasks, too. I'm exhilarated when I go to a funeral and discover the service was planned by the person now dead. That realization can startle in the moment; it can also inspire. Such focused courage may prompt us to shed our usual passivity about death and instead participate in shaping our own last acts.

Whenever someone—either at the time of dying or long before—insists on a frank reckoning with death, they encourage us to forego the idea that life and death inhabit separate realms. We normally cherish life and reject whatever threatens it, but our very cherishing can also block acknowledgement that death lives in every breath we take. The older we get, the more this consciousness bears down on us—often matched by the impulse to snap off the consciousness, like an unwelcome light.

Consider how we are liable to react if the subject of death comes up in public conversation. It's a rare event, but it happens. We tend to swerve away. We might titter a bit or get tongue-tied, as though we've just bumped into an off-color joke. We definitely skirt specific talk about obituaries and tombstones. We may express a collective hope that family or friends will handle these particulars when the time comes, and someone might remark, "Well, I'll be gone; it won't matter." Perhaps it won't. Tackling these necessities ourselves, though, and facing into the wind we know will inevitably blow for us, brings various benefits, besides sparing people we love some doleful chores.

For one thing, embracing end-of-life tasks, and making plain we're doing so, can create collective meaning— especially for others in the tunnel of old age. We encourage bravery by pointing directly at the subject we'd all rather avoid. We also strengthen people coming behind us, children and grandchildren seeking guidance on this mighty issue, as we too perhaps sought when younger. Clearly, someone flush with life will not be able to pay serious attention to talk of death. Almost by definition, they aren't supposed to. Nevertheless, if we can approach death by becoming "fierce with reality," as an old expression goes, we'll not only embolden ourselves but perhaps fortify those who will be helping to usher us out.

Mary Oliver, in her poem, "When Death Comes," suggests why a measure of fierceness matters:

When it's over, I don't want to wonder
if I have made of my life something particular, and real.
I don't want to find myself sighing and frightened, or
full of argument.
I don't want to end up simply having visited this world.

We might secretly feel we *have* largely been a visitor or

that we've tamped down some of our vitality. Even so, at the end, assuming we are not utterly incapacitated or witless, we can choose to meet death with our own version of bravery and perhaps shift things from timid to powerful.

Once upon a time, I masterfully evaded the subject of death. It wasn't until I spent years as a clergywoman in the Episcopal Church, dealing with death close-up, that I found a more courageous perch. And, like most of us, I had to be dragged onto that perch by the grappling hooks of experience. One such hook, for me, was conducting funerals.

The prayers for burial in the Episcopal *Book of Common Prayer* contain some jarring words. Whenever I had to recite these ancient prayers, I could hear the quiver in my own voice. "All we go down to the dust, yet even at the grave we make our song: Alleluia, alleluia, alleluia."

I've had many people tell me that phrase causes them to cry. I agree; it can make both speaker and listener shudder. Of course, it's partly a shudder of relief. The very fact of being at a funeral suggests we're unlikely, at least on that day, to go down to the dust ourselves. But there's more to it. Reciting an alleluia at the lip of the grave makes our hearts quake because the words are bold and defiant. For a brief moment our prayer declares, in unison, that life is more powerful than death. No wonder we quake.

Some of my most compelling experiences in ministry occurred when I was called to look death in the eye and somehow find that alleluia. I had to find one when I buried a stillborn baby in a lonely corner of a cemetery, the single mother clutching a bouquet of white lilies as she watched her girl go into the ground. I had to find another when I went to search out a ninety-two-year-old I'd made pastoral visits to for years, as she lay on a slab in a crematory anteroom. When I raised my hand to her craggy cheek, cold as marble, the alleluia came hard. It also did when I had to do a memorial service for the only child of middle-aged parents, gone with a sudden illness. Taxing as these and many similar experiences were, I am bone grateful for them, for their complexity. They were painful—and bracing. They were heartbreaking—and radically formative. And all the meaning they held, the harsh and the tender, is now laced through whatever quotient of courage I've mustered for my own end.

But there's a strange irony in this. Such courage can only flourish if it moves in and out of awareness. If I were continually conscious of the human anguish signified by those final alleluias, my courage would evaporate. Just as sanity would flee if I fixated on time passing, minute to minute. At the end of our lives, on any day, facing into the wind of our approaching death depends on living creatively with two opposing truths: death is coming on a hard-charging horse, *and* the horse has not arrived in the yard yet. He will eventually be there, snorting and carrying on. But he isn't here in this moment. The question is, can we hold both of these truths close—first one, then the other—and deal bravely with the ambiguities created by each.

Usually we'd rather ignore the darker side of the picture. Death doesn't get much of our direct attention. We may not plug our ears and hum, but mostly we *don't want to hear about it.* Even though we know better, we hope the horse will just ride eternally off into some other yard.

Holding life and death together is a primal tension that human beings have grappled with forever. And there's at least one reason this tension will never vanish: we know our own death is inevitable and yet, simultaneously, it feels impossible. Our death is the truest truth—and in the same instant it seems like a lie. We believe the truth, and then we un-believe it. We have opined, along with countless others, "Oh, everything dies," but we also famously keep our fingers crossed behind our backs.

The older we get, the starker the oncoming truth of our death reveals itself to be. Awareness we might still have successfully blurred out in mid-life or early old age now gets clearer. The Law of Averages starts to show up everywhere. We encounter more frequent illness in those we know; more people close to us begin to die. And with each succeeding death, our own death inches nearer. Likewise, the thought of our closest relationships coming to an end begins to weigh heavily. The prospect causes acute anguish when those relationships are dear and perhaps a tinge of guilty relief when they are fraught.

This process gets fast-tracked when we learn, or re-learn, of grave illness in someone, not necessarily an intimate. Recently I was in the supermarket, picking out onions and potatoes, when I ran into a woman I've known tangentially all my life. She is a little older than I am, and we share a certain wry approach to aging. On this day, though, all wryness was drowned in the Niagara of tears that began pouring down her cheeks when we met up. I suspected her husband, sick for a couple of years, must be worse. I soon heard it was true: the treatment he'd been receiving had stopped working. The length of time they'd both hoped for had suddenly shortened, by a lot.

Besides the experience of fellow suffering, an encounter that plunges us into someone else's fears about death can also move the dial on our own standoff with it. The shadow falls a little closer. The kaleidoscope shifts, rearranging the colored fragments. The rope tightens in the tug-of-war between our awareness of death and our evasion of it.

Whatever the circumstances of such an encounter, we'll probably be tempted to bolt. We might leap into prattle about an unrelated subject, or develop a sudden need for the bathroom, or remember an urgent phone call—anything to relieve the anxiety. Those moves are understandable; I've made them all myself. And yet, I like to think an upwelling of courage will help us reach for a deeper response, that we'll find the nerve to turn *toward* the heartache right in front of us, as bravely as we are able.

In a completely different context, one of the best illustrations of such turning was told to me long ago by my father. When serving in the Army during World War II, he had been much affected by stories he heard of bagpipers *choosing* to heft their instruments onto their shoulders and march defiantly out onto the battlefields of Europe: men of Scotland, Ireland, Canada, pennants flapping and songs unleashed, horns blaring into the very ears of death. Although this is a long way from a chance meeting with a distraught acquaintance in a grocery aisle, both experiences fall on the continuum of how we face death. And both are about choices.

We each have our small, homegrown opportunities for courage when the specter of death surfaces nearby. It's courageous to stand still, right there by the onions, and not seek refuge in small talk. It's courageous to devote one's spirit, however briefly, to another person's anguish. It's courageous to acknowledge how puny, cracked, and fickle our frail humanity can be when reckoning with the power of death.

But such courage is exacting. Our hearts will beat harder when we decline an escape hatch, when we hang in with someone else's distressing proximity to death. Whoever said *courage is fear that has said its prayers* was right: in settings where we summon even a demitasse of bravery, fear will be in the next sip.

At best, our attempts to face into the wind will probably come up short, and be bold one moment, faltering the next. My own half-baked accomplishments are proof positive. Various pieces of a funeral service now sit, still disconnected, on my desk. The stone markers we bought for the island cemetery finally migrated to the four corners of the plot, but only after they sat on top of our woodpile for two years. I've written scraps of my obituary; it wouldn't take much of a breeze across my desk to scatter them. Tom and I agreed to the design for a gravestone, but haven't ordered it from the monument company, much less arranged for it to be engraved with partial information and sunk into the ground. That task awaits another Maine summer, maybe this summer coming up...

And as for that pile of old shoes on my closet floor? They are still in a heap, collecting good intentions.

Downcast

When my two younger sisters and I were growing up, we used to play at being nuns. We practiced walking rigidly straight, heavy books on our heads. We trained our eyes on the ground, striving for nun perfection. And we invented holy orders, like Little Servants of the Savior, conjuring the delicious privations we associated with lives of selflessness and devotion. Never mind that we were usually devoted to nothing more pious than a hearty lunch and a spin on our bikes; the game of downcast eyes amused us.

Such amusement was a long way back when I reached my late seventies and realized that keeping my eyes trained on the ground was pivotal to preserving life and limb. A couple of fancy falls did the trick. One occurred as I motored at battle speed across the smooth painted floor of our kitchen, in stocking feet, went down hard, and was rewarded with busted ribs. Another happened when I tripped on an uneven brick sidewalk in Portland, eyes ahead rather than down, all nuns a distant memory. I landed splat, grinding my glasses into my face. A day later, raccoon eyes bloomed as advertisements of my folly.

Either of those headlong spills could have borne out the obituary line, "She died from complications of a fall." Uh huh. It was only when that thought focused itself like a homing pigeon, though, that I began to see what I had to do. And not just sometimes. All the time: look down.

Easy to say, hard to pull off. At least for me. It feels so oppressive, so anti-myself. It means not flying around, a life-long mode of behavior that caused my family to nickname me Crash. But I know what I'm *doing* when I'm in motion—or like to think I do. Clearly that flattering self-image is on its way out. Plunging forward may be fine for a ten-year old girl on a bike. Not so fine if the girl still lives, untamed, in the woman staring at her 80th birthday on the near horizon.

Slowing down, looking down, demands a peculiar constancy of awareness. It also involves tacit consent to place risk on top of the consciousness pile. Minimization of risk, after all, is a chief reason people go into assisted living facilities, counting on features like wall-to-wall carpeting, elevators, doorsills level with floors—everything designed to vastly lower the chances of tripping or falling.

Since we've chosen to remain in our house on the island rather than decamp to an assisted living facility, I have to up the ante on myself and try to maintain constant vigilance when moving around the world. Such non-stop focus is problematic. I may have gained in my struggle against a headstrong nature, but a distracted split second is all it takes to be embraced by a floor or a sidewalk. Or a boat dock. Living on an island that involves a ferry ride, I've made intimate acquaintance with the uneven planks of a dock more than once.

Obviously, the physical cost of this can be high. The emotional cost, though, may be just as high and accompanied by a measure of grief, no matter how masked. For instance, when an old person falls, they are likely to be flooded with chagrin, an emotion which fuses aggravation, shame, and a subtle grief. Falling amplifies a sense of diminished capacity that's probably already underway. I suspect this is why, in a public fall, that older person may protest, "Oh, I'm fine!" to whatever phalanx of concerned onlookers comes running. Even when blood is spurting from a wound, there's a strong urge to minimize, to beat back the chagrin. If we're gradually losing the ability to remain vertical, and we despise admitting it, a fall may prompt us to tartly declare that we're in command when we're not. We're also unlikely to acknowledge the dejection a fall can produce.

Related emotional costs occur when nimble feet turn clumsy. A current tendency to stumble makes me feel as though a demon slinks ahead of me, opening cupboard doors to smack my forehead, fabricating obstacles out of thin air. Having two left feet particularly torments the dancer who still lives in me. I learned to dance when I was about seven, and came to almost prefer dancing to eating. That extra left foot would have been an utter stranger to me at the island square dances I once so loved, or on the

Israeli kibbutz of my early adulthood, where wildly intricate folk dances could electrify me until midnight turned to morning. Those dancing days are long over, but my feet hold indelible memories, and my heart still hears old music. This means stumbling can provoke exasperation and also faint sorrow.

Of course, a younger person might say that addressing this clumsiness and diminished capacity is simple: just quit arguing with the facts, and send yesterday to the cleaners. Buy a snazzy walking stick! Wear a call button! Roll up the Oriental rugs! None of that is bad advice. It's reasonable to be extra prudent after vaulting the bar, so to speak, into one's seventies. But what someone younger doesn't understand (and I believe *can't* understand because it isn't clear until a certain age) is the emotional loss obscured by the reasonable advice.

Take the seemingly simple example of a person long accustomed to stacking his or her own firewood, like my husband. Once upon a few short years ago, when we got our annual four cords of split wood delivered to the side yard, Tom would spend a couple of spring afternoons contentedly laying up logs into rows he knew would not collapse under high winds or heavy snow. The work satisfied a number of physical and emotional needs: it kept him out in the fresh air; he could happily conjure the frigid days when the woodstove in our living room would give us great comfort; he relished the strength of body and spirit attached to his self-sufficiency.

Year after year, on those sweet spring afternoons, diminished capacities were a distant concern. Now, with both of us in our late seventies, we've quit arguing with the facts and have hired a teenaged boy to stack the wood. It seems as though this should be a relief to Tom. It is. And that he would enjoy a younger person handling the task. He does. And he doesn't. Surrendering the work brings deliverance; it also brings a certain melancholy that, while perhaps outwardly muted, can still be keenly felt.

This kind of loss, or the specter of it, may go unnoticed—except through someone's quiet rebellion against restraint. For years, a weather-beaten old fisherman was our neighbor and friend. In his early nineties, in biting cold weather, he could still be found outside continuing to split wood and stack it. All the while leaning on his walker. Did his wife make a hollering fuss? She did. But she also knew that if her fear of his risk made him quit doing what he *could* do, a portion of the meaning in his life would evaporate like morning mist off the beach in front of their house. His stubbornness and unorthodox use of the walker may have riled others' expectations, but his vitality was tied up with defying those very expectations. Whether his defiance shortened his life, I'm not sure. But I am sure that if he had stopped this sort of work, the books he might have added to his already sagging bookshelf would have failed to fully satisfy his spirit. Once he relinquished *his own version of physical work that also met his emotional needs,* he had to know his last log was about to be stacked.

Tom is perhaps more ready than this neighbor to admit the limitations of aging. But he's not that ready. He

resists shifting into the constraints of an "older" consciousness, as do I. The reason is straightforward: that shift
signals movement from having autonomy to losing it. It
heralds a push, almost imperceptible, but a push nonethe-
less, toward the day when we'll exert far less control over
our own lives than we do now. On the surface this involves stopping certain types of physical work, but underneath it's about emotional loss. It means admitting that
competencies we once cherished are either going or gone,
leaving us with the thorny issue of how we are going to
adjust to their departure.

I think of my father-in-law in relation to that adjust-
ment. Though he earned a living for over fifty years as a
university professor of theology, he also set great store by
his physical capacities and derived much meaning from
their use. He restored furniture, repaired antiques, directed the building or renovation of houses for his family.
But a time came in the labor on one of those houses when
he conceded the straw bossing to Tom, then in his strap-
ping young thirties and already shouldering the heavy lifting on the project. The father, who had formerly sweated
and strained alongside his son in many physically strenuous settings, became the assistant. He was now the person
who fetched the hammer and saw; he no longer wielded
them much. A few years back I saw a similar hand-off
when our middle-aged son-in-law tackled a building task
at our house and Tom ferried him the necessary tools instead of piling into the job himself, as he once would have
done with great gusto.

Change of this sort usually happens slowly, like summer slipping into fall. The note of sadness in it may be little more than a whisper, making the emotional cost easy to miss. That could partly explain why much of the conversation about aging in modern American culture is not about emotional complexity. Nor does the wistfulness that older people can experience get much attention. Talk tends, instead, to be upbeat, to focus on physical aspects of aging, specifically about delaying those. We're exhorted to keep walking, keep swimming, keep carrying on with whatever activity will preserve physical fitness.

All that activity may well result in physical *and* emotional gains. At the same time, if you are older, you are older. And you know it. No cheerleading to the contrary will change things. And you know it. Being older doesn't mean we have to stop walking or swimming; if anything, aging might give us more zeal for staying active. Nevertheless. Older people have also become wryly familiar with handwriting on a wall still invisible to those younger: *the decline of your capacities is at hand.* That isn't exactly a signboard proclaiming The End is Nigh, but an older person knows the guy with the sign hanging around his neck is standing on a street corner right nearby.

Which raises a question. Can we have heightened awareness of growing older, with its attendant losses, and not become depressed? It's a double-edged sword. Staying conscious of our aging, while it's happening to us, feels hard. It may depress us. And if we insist on going *un*conscious about it that will also depress us.

It's a bit like the process at any age of being angry with someone. Unresolved, the feelings just won't quit; the burn intensifies. If we stay conscious of our anger, we may eventually decide to walk the difficult road of voicing it. No matter what, though, until we get around to speaking up, the prospect of the conversation is depressing. And if we stuff the anger down, as many of us have discovered to our dismay, this too will depress us.

If staying conscious of our anger is problematic, how much more daunting it is to realize that the river of mortality is rolling ever faster underneath us, and we should smarten up about certain things. Like heightening our awareness of potentially deadly threats, such as falling.

When I declared a few pages back that, in trying to prevent a fall, it was impossible to keep ourselves constantly focused on the ground, it wasn't quite right. It would have been more accurate to say that this constancy is extremely difficult to pull off because it's not just a "good idea." It's not a theory, or an optional memory exercise, or a well-intentioned promise to keep our eyes directed downward when doing so happens to occur to us.

Instead, in crucial contrast, this degree of consciousness involves repeatedly making real for ourselves the *awful experience* of falling. It demands permanent commitment to the ugly details of previous falls. It means maintaining a cocked awareness for the stuttering footwork we know occurs in the instant before going down. It commits us to keeping that about-to-fall sensation alive, being willing to re-live the dreaded feeling of your foot about to clip the edge of the rug. It means letting yourself hear again—and again—the sickening sound of your forehead hitting the brick or the plank.

We dodge this super-awareness, in part, because remembering those pre-seconds, imprinting them, hanging onto them, is very unpleasant. We rush to erase the repellent memory as fast we can. But to stay conscious, we have to insist on keeping those memories fresh. Obviously, we can't do so every second of the day—in our own house or out in the world. We'd never leave the living room couch. And mere determination *not* to fall won't prevent us from doing so. But the point stands: there's a profound difference between a fleeting resolution and a soul-embedded decision to remain deeply conscious of a commitment.

There's little doubt that this level of focused constancy will leave a trace of depression. I know because I'm currently attempting that constancy myself. And it's not strange that a bit of depression seeps in; the process involves losing a certain carefreeness we enjoyed for many years.

Despite that lamentable thought, this doesn't have to involve a change of personality. I was born with a carefree heart and will probably die with one. It does mean waving goodbye to that ten-year old girl on the bike, and calling to her disappearing figure, "I'm so glad to have known you!" Actually, I'm amazed to have known her. But if I hope to greet next Tuesday without a fresh crop of black eyes and bruises, I have to reach for something new. Not the new of being young, but of being old. Which involves a very different kind of amazement—likely to be accompanied by at least a muted strain of the blues.

Vanishing Act

I was twenty-one when my mother asked if I wanted to join her in taking care of my grandmother, her mother, for the summer. It was a good offer: living on the island at my parents' house, being a light duty caregiver and companion to someone I loved dearly. I would be paid by my aunt and uncle, with whom my grandmother normally lived; my mother intimated they needed a reprieve. I wasn't sure why a reprieve from such a mild, unassuming, elderly woman might be in order, but I quickly said I'd do it.

With such youthful enthusiasm and innocence, my acquaintance with dementia began. I barely knew the word when I agreed to the plan. In the fifty-plus years since that distant summer, the word has never left my awareness. The singular darkness of the disease fell over me during those weeks, generating a long line of future fears. Some of the fears were realized; others became grey shadows hiding ever since in the brush along the road. At twenty-one, I had no idea how relentless and cruel dementia is for both sufferer and witnesses. It seemed to me then, furthermore, that a caregiver had only one reasonable course of action: befriending the affliction.

My grandmother had never been a big reader, but she loved being read to. Soon after she arrived on the island, she and I developed a pattern of taking chairs and a book to the shade of the back lawn on fair days. Only partially able to focus on a story, she seemed content with summery airs, birdsong, and the sound of my voice. There was an old-fashioned sweetness to our companionship as she settled in to the routines of the house. She also exuded a kind of grateful reserve. She didn't say much when we ate, or when she rocked in her chair on the porch, or took walks with me—very quiet walks.

It took me a couple of days to figure out that my grandmother had gone mostly silent. I'd always experienced her as a merry soul with a quietly mischievous sense of humor, and she did still show traces of that spirit. Now, though, she seemed shrouded in silence. After a while I realized, also, that her silence had a certain flat quality. It wasn't restful, or reflective; it felt vacant. If I asked her a question, she might give a limited response, but she almost never initiated any talk. In other words, she seemed to lack "agency", or the independent capacity to start a conversation.

She tipped me off further when she didn't ask about cooking. She had always been a first-rate cook and had taught me many useful culinary tricks. In the past, if she and I were together at my mother's house on the island, we happily concocted pies and puddings using those tricks. Now, when I asked her to cook with me, she seemed anxious or perplexed. Or blank. No matter how I tried to coax out her interest, I struck no chord. She might smile at me, but there wasn't any depth to the creases around her mouth—only the same curious flatness. I would later learn this was a hallmark of dementia.

The flatness unnerved me, but I didn't want to admit it. Especially not to my mother. She and I had traveled many rocky emotional roads since my childhood, and I was loath to introduce any new boulders. I was determined to make the arrangement succeed.

Because my father was working in New York City and only came home to the island on weekends, my mother's growing exasperation found little relief. I regularly urged her out of the house to go sailing, thinking it would fortify her humor and my own. It became obvious after about a week, however, that her patience was wearing thin. In retrospect, I believe she was frightened. From telephone conversations I overheard her having with my aunt and uncle, she knew the deterioration she was seeing in her mother had been *their* daily fare for some time. But she was new to it. As the reality sank in, my mother's fear rose, and so did her temper.

It was no big surprise, then, roughly two weeks after my grandmother arrived, to be wakened in the middle of the night by a commotion coming from the bathroom. My mother was yelling. When I arrived on the scene, my grandmother stood blinking in the bathroom doorway. A glance told the tale: she had put on all five of the house-dresses she'd arrived with, one on top of the other. In be-tween blinks she was whimpering, trying to say that she thought it was morning. This cut no mustard with my mother, which made me furious, and of course I said so. Big boulder. After some heavy breathing, I managed to get my grandmother back into her room, swap all the dresses for a nightgown, reinstall her in bed, and return to my own.

When morning came, my mother and I avoided the subject of our crossed wires. But once I had delivered my grandmother (in a single dress) to the breakfast table, my mother's pointed queries to her about the midnight events, which my grandmother didn't remember, made the situa-tion plain. My aunt and uncle might need a vacation, but my mother's capacity to provide one was swiftly unravel-ing. And protests to her in private about my being the bearing beam and wanting to finish out the summer fell on mostly deaf ears.

The final bell tolled a few days later. My father was home for the weekend, and the four of us were at the din-ner table. My grandmother was her usual quiet self, seem-ingly unperturbed. Then, without preamble, she stood up from the table. She announced with some urgency that she "had to go down to the beach to meet Rob," her husband, dead now for twenty years. She floundered toward a din-ing room window, mistaking it for the door to the porch, and made motions to climb through it. Catching my mother's face aflame with anguish, I jumped up to steer my grandmother toward the door. As she and I descended the porch steps, I heard my mother's wail, declaring to my father that she was at the end of her rope.

Among other agonies, I think my mother couldn't bear to see the memory of her much-beloved father exhumed for an imaginary tryst on the beach. Not only had she lost him, but now she was losing her mother, too—still present in body, but long gone in mind. Soon after that evening, my aunt and uncle agreed we'd terminate the plan. And soon after *that*, my grandmother was installed in a nursing home, a place she ever after referred to as The Bughouse when she sent us her sad, unintelligible letters.

Jump forward roughly thirty years, long after my mother had been widowed and then re-married. I was playing Scrabble with her one afternoon when she heaved a loud, exasperated sigh. She was having trouble forming the letters into intelligible words, she told me, and admitted it had happened before. Since she was a gifted Scrabble player, who relished any match of linguistic wits, the idea that her game could stray toward gibberish felt menacing—to her, and certainly to me.

A related incident followed some days later. As she lay reading on her living room couch, with me in the kitchen nearby, she indignantly announced to the universe that she had just read the same sentence half a dozen times and still couldn't follow what was going on in her book. My mother was a champion reader. Not only had books been a chief pleasure all her life, but reading provided some of the strongest stitches that bound her psyche together.

These signs of trouble weren't the first. For months, the multiple notes she strewed around her house had given my sisters and me pause. They were written in a wavery script—handwriting reminiscent of my grandmother's letters from The Bughouse. Finding these notes, sometimes in peculiar locations, I felt as though I were following Hansel and Gretel's trail. Their breadcrumbs, though, had obvious meaning. These notes often didn't, or didn't to anyone other than my mother and perhaps my stepfather.

Indeed, for quite a while by then, he had seemed to be working double time to keep my mother afloat. It was a subtle art. He would take over, for instance, when she was trying to open a can of soup, his smooth actions making an onlooker wonder whether he was just being helpful, or knew she was having trouble figuring out how the can opener worked.

Shortly after he died, that question was inarguable. She didn't understand can openers or a great many other things. This was a woman who once operated mostly solo—wiring lamps, tackling the work on her sailboat, wallpapering bedrooms. Those capacities had atrophied years earlier, but the spirit she projected late into her life remained one of fierce competence and independence. That wasn't the truth about her anymore; it was the truth she wanted to believe.

Once our stepfather was gone from her side, his pivotal role in her moment to moment living became clear. He wasn't just the other half of their equation; she was mostly lost without him. My sisters and I decided that, for the moment, she needed to live with one of us. Accordingly, she embarked on a lengthy sojourn with my sister down on Cape Cod. This continued until she became hell-bent to return to her house on the island, insisting she would live alone, with Tom and me a few miles down the road.

Once she returned, her confusion and lostness became evident pretty fast. The truth of it finally landed with a thud for me when I went to her house one morning and found her sitting in the kitchen, staring at a radio. "What is this thing?" she asked me. When I told her, with a disbelieving half laugh, that it was a radio, she said, "But what is it for?" The laugh died in my throat. Her days of living alone were over.

Almost overnight, my mother moved into the assisted living facility on the island. It was a fight to keep her there; the dementia had convinced her she was being held prisoner. And in a sense, she was. The place is an old-fashioned farmhouse, not a locked facility; its porous boundaries made her think she could breach them whenever she chose. Which she regularly did. And was just as regularly rounded up by the staff and brought back, reinforcing the feeling of being imprisoned.

In addition, given her decades-long familiarity with

the island, and despite the dementia, she was aware of the short distance between the assisted living facility and her own house. This knowledge haunted her. When she heard thunder, for example, she would insist she needed to go home and shut her windows. If no one was right there to dissuade her, she would streak out the door—intent on walking briskly toward a task that she would never again perform, in a house that would never again be hers.

It took only about six weeks for her tenure at the facility to disintegrate. Tom and I tried to soften her mounting distress by taking her on frequent rides, picnicking in her favorite island haunts, and bringing her often to our house for dinner. But any gains were short lived. She couldn't get past the sensation of being a prisoner, which made her increasingly angry. And combative.

One evening while at our house for supper, she decided we too were keeping her captive. She bolted from the kitchen. As I caught up with her at the end of the driveway and reached to restrain her, she bit hard into my arm. That bite was furious, frantic, crazed. And it sank far down into my lofty idea from decades earlier that the caregiver's principal task was befriending the dementia. I knew this was still true in the broadest sense. But my mother's deranged state caused memories of our long-ago mutual suffering over *her* mother's disintegration to flood back through me. With both of us watered by her racking sobs, those memories now bloomed in far more complex colors, as my very sore arm gathered her toward me in a new forgiveness.

. . .

With this history, one might ask whether I'm tempted to strap bricks to my feet and jump off the nearest bridge. Heredity, after all, speaks with a loud voice on the subject of dementia. And yet that voice also delivers a choice. On the one hand, I need to acknowledge a mother and a grandmother vanquished by the disease. On the other hand—perhaps the far more important one—I need to live as though I'm going to outrun this affliction. That may seem like wishful thinking. But it isn't inevitable I'll be caught by dementia; it's only a harrowing possibility.

The back and forth of that is tricky. For instance, I can vow fear of the disease will not rule my spirit. But the vow starts to wobble when, in a baffling move, I stash my cosmetic bag in the refrigerator. I later can't find the bag. Naturally, I don't look in the refrigerator because what ninny would put it there?

Or there's the morning on the ferry dock when I mistake someone else's car for ours. It's not until I am loading my gear into the back of his car and hear the approaching owner's amused query that I realize my error. Funny? Briefly. Not funny that it required his voice to regain my wits.

And then there was the recent day I was oh-so-carefully separating six eggs to make a cake, and oh-so-carefully dropped the sixth yolk into the bowl of whites, ruining my effort.

It's a great temptation to draw a line from dementia in one generation to dementia in the next, as though a map conclusively pointed. But as someone once said, a map is never the country itself, it's just ink suggesting a possible route.

I work to keep that distinction straight. To expressly remind myself of the occasions when I separate the eggs without error, approach the correct car, put the cosmetic bag away where it belongs. Day to day, I live in that clear-headed territory. Which is no doubt why my family thinks I'm nuts to fret. I'm writing these essays, aren't I? And I believe I'm many miles distant from precincts where radios aren't recognizable—if the map ever leads me there at all.

I'm mostly successful, in other words, in holding anxiety about dementia at bay. And yet. I recall a phone conversation with my mother, well before the end of her days, when she remarked with great agitation, *I can't tell you the number of stupid things I do now.* She didn't like to elaborate on her missteps, so I didn't ask what she was talking about. An egg yolk in the wrong bowl? I wonder.

News From the Future

We didn't immediately notice it was missing. One minute I was watching our skiff bob along behind us in the churning ocean wake. The next time I checked it was gone, the line trailing slack off the stern.

Through the roar of the engine, I grabbed Tom's arm to signal my distress. He looked back over his shoulder and yelled, "Where the hell is it?" He cut the engine. We scanned the water behind us, far out to the distant ocean. Nothing. All we saw was the hulking shape of Seguin Island a few miles back, its dark green outline backlit by the bright sun and scudding midday clouds. We had steered clear of a nasty reef as we passed Seguin; now we worried that the wooden skiff might be headed for a harsh fate on that same reef.

We were on the first leg of a junket down the Maine coast in our sleep-aboard lobster boat, a trip we'd made many times before. When we realized the skiff was gone, we were roughly three hours from home. We had another three to go before we reached that afternoon's destination. The smaller boat was a crucial feature of these ventures. For one thing, it gave us a means of potential self-rescue out on the ocean in the unlikely event we had to abandon the large boat. We knew that in seriously bad weather this would be a last-ditch proposition, but the backup still offered a certain dim comfort.

Secondly, though, the skiff allowed us to move around easily whenever we anchored. We used it to motor through harbors, travel in shallow water, find repair materials, or food and wine, and go into a marina for a shower. Barring an ocean-going disaster, having the skiff wasn't crucial. But losing it would put a big kink in our usual pleasures.

Tom powered up the engine, swung the boat in a wide arc, and headed back toward Seguin. Steam was coming out his ears at the likelihood he'd gotten distracted and tied a faulty knot in the line. Although he hadn't fully acknowledged it to me yet, I knew this would not be his first experience of distraction when on the boat. And he feared becoming forgetful. The fear was muted, but we both understood that persistent absentmindedness on his part would end our ocean adventures.

Drawing near Seguin and still seeing no sign of the skiff, Tom decided to phone the Coast Guard. When he finally raised them, they told him a lobsterman had picked up a small boat, adrift. They offered to bring it to us, with a warning that we'd need to prove it was ours. We had the necessary papers. Once a new knot was secured and copious thanks bestowed on the Coast Guard, we were on our way down east again in high spirits—albeit with a crimp in our self-assurance.

It took a couple more seasons of cruising down the coast for that crimp to become a real dent. And it wasn't a dent that affected Tom alone, as captain. It cut into the confidence we felt as a team. Taken separately, the cues were negligible: a valve left unclosed, a gauge misread, a hose incorrectly attached, all easy to shrug off as simple errors. Combined, though, they were omens that made noise. Faint but persistent noise.

Equally important, as the years ticked by and the boat trips continued, we both felt our energy and physical capacity decreasing. We were still plenty fit as we approached our mid-seventies, but a lobster boat is a large-scale undertaking. Everything about it is big: the size, the amount of heavy maintenance required, and the regular operating tasks. It all takes muscle. Forgetfulness and faulty knots were real concerns, but declining vigor also emerged as a pressing issue.

Then there were the emotional hints. It slowly crept over us, for example, that we had become more anxious about fog. Even when we anchored in the harbor where Tom had spent many summers as a boy—on a waterway he once zipped through in his outboard, blithe to weather fair or foul—he had now begun to look askance at fog when it rolled in off the ocean. Both of us balked at leaving the shelter of a familiar refuge to test ourselves against it.

Though we had never welcomed fog when on the boat, an earlier spirit of derring-do was replaced by hesitancy. Like a kind of emotional malware, consciousness of aging now infected our nerve. We were not surprised by a sense of advancing vulnerability since we didn't begin these jaunts until our late sixties. But we were dismayed.

Although he had owned many boats in his life, Tom saved a big piece of his heart for a lobster boat and, once he found her, poured enormous energy into reclaiming her. For a while, he explored the waters close to home, rejoicing in extending the boundaries of our island life out to the open ocean.

His dream, though, was to go down east with me—gunkholing, as it's sometimes called, meandering along the coastline, going from cove to cove, sleeping aboard, and exploring unfamiliar shores. After doing this for a couple of weeks each summer, over many years, time together on the boat gathered real importance and meaning for us both. She was a ticket to leisure we could afford, a freedom we reveled in. Simultaneously, over those same years, the boat became a family pleasure. The grandchildren, always eager to fish when aboard, came to relish taking picnics to deserted islands and vagabonding around the bay where we live.

It was against this background that the skiff gave us the slip that sunny morning. Its disappearance on a bad knot—a knot Tom had been tying correctly his entire life—lengthened a shadow for us both. News of an expiration date for our watery sojourns was traveling toward us.

The reckoning still came slowly, especially for me. I had a hard time digesting the idea that age might be compromising our safety. I was used to thinking of Tom as exceptionally deft when on the water. I'd watched him sling so many anchors with aplomb, pilot the boat in ridiculously tight situations, skirt disaster and come out the other side grinning. I couldn't imagine those capacities, like the skiff, could be sliding out of view.

Slowly, however, they were. And before long, other concerns arose. Such as balance, an older person's plague. Especially on a boat. Most of the time, when conditions were calm, balance still didn't claim much of our attention. But if the wind blew hard or tricky maneuvers were called for up on the bow in rough water, the need for surefootedness snapped into focus. Tom's intermittent balance problems caused particular concern because the deck work fell to him. With some similar troubles of my own, *his* balance then became a joint safety pre-occupation.

Other questions also cropped up, like what we'd do if one of us fell overboard. We were both decent swimmers but knew that even our combined energies wouldn't haul us back up into the boat; we simply weren't strong enough anymore. That awareness prompted us to fasten a sturdy bronze ladder onto the stern, a precaution which didn't really erase the anxiety. Despite having a ladder, falling overboard in a variety of challenging circumstances could send at least one of us down to Davy Jones' Locker. Finally, the news was conclusive: not only was our energy waning, but we were spending far more time rattled about safety issues than we were savoring life on the bounding main. It was time to quit.

It might seem as though surrendering our years-long pleasure and putting the boat up for sale would bring on nothing but sadness. And there was plenty of that. We were sad about losing this particular freedom, sorry about the secluded coastal havens we'd loved and wouldn't see again. There's a kind of cloistered and delicious existence only found on a boat; we would sorely miss it. We were also regretful for the rest of the family. Giving up the boat would take a significant bite out of their fun when on the island and constrict our collective summer pleasures.

Despite those real losses, though, the chief emotion we experienced was not regret but relief. The boat's physical demands had become a heavy burden for Tom. He loved her dearly, and every year his affection was more heavily taxed by the energy required to maintain her. Like the contest with safety issues, age got pitted against his work capacity, and age was gaining ground each season.

In short, we were glad the boat sold. But it was a complicated gladness. She was bought by a guy from down the coast, someone we could tell was going to enjoy her as much as we had. That made us happy—and of course the actual deed was flavored with strong rue.

As Tom said when I asked him how he felt on the morning the boat was finally gone, "I'm only glad because I know I can't do the work anymore. It's someone else's turn." The pleasure of leaping from bed early on a spring morning to repair and paint was over. Now the pleasure lay in *not* having to do that. But the "not having to," when older, is a double-edged sword.

When something stops being easy, continuing to do it creates stress, strain, and discouragement. In this case, however, it also meant the end of a passionate project, bidding an ambivalent goodbye to a pursuit that gave enormous emotional and physical satisfaction for years— which had only been brought to a stop by the vagaries of aging. It was another lesson in understanding that all our lives we are only stewards of whatever we cherish, not owners.

On an evening soon after the sale, we walked down to the cove near our house where the boat had always been moored with a small fleet of others, mostly lobster boats, sometimes an occasional sailboat. The sun was going down, throwing its gold and vermilion streaks wide across the sky. For years it had been our delight to walk there on just this sort of evening, to look at the boat, to relish her role in our lives, and to imagine future trips.

Now our mooring buoy was still on the far side of the cove, but beside it was a hole in the water. Seeing that empty place was hard, and yet we had to admit the sight was also welcome. It was gladness in reverse—looking through and beyond the vacant spot to a pleasure that had come to us in its own good time, then departed, leaving blessing in its wake. Losses and gains were rolled together: we were the richer for it all.

A Glimpse of Grace

Every year Tom and I travel to a pastoral corner of Vermont to visit a cemetery that is physically beautiful and spiritually stirring. We go in October, the season for buying big baskets of chrysanthemums to place on his family's graves. It's the month the white hydrangea blossoms in the cemetery are fading to soft rust. It's also when "crimson flames from autumn hills," as Tom's beloved paternal grandfather, now under that Vermont ground for sixty years, once wrote in a poem about the mountains ringing the cemetery. We go, in other words, during a season—and to a place—alive with poignancy.

Some of that poignancy arises from my memory of Tom first bringing me to the cemetery on a June day early in our relationship, almost forty years ago. Heady with the scent of lilacs and wrapped in sweet kisses, we rolled around the grassy slopes, full of hope that when we married, we would create a baby, further extending the family tree deeply rooted there. But it didn't happen; no baby of our own ever came. Each visit we've made, though, since the initial one, has been colored for me by that long-ago lovers' tumble and its mingled tastes of life and death.

Still more poignancy springs from our being the ministers at graveside services held here for Tom's mother, father, and brother, dying in three terrible successive years. His clergyman brother was with us to help bury each parent. A few short months later, Tom and I stood together looking down into that brother's fresh grave.

Almost thirty years have passed since those interments. We were still young enough, back then, to hold mortality out of focus. Now, both careening toward eighty, the lens on mortality is highly polished. Awareness of life's fleetingness has moved much further down in our bones. And when we perch on the granite tombstones, Mt. Equinox towering behind us, smoke from autumn leaves burning nearby carries an unmistakable question. How many more Octobers will we come here with our baskets of flowers? And then the other question too painful to ask, let alone answer. Would either of us come here alone?

I believe Tom would eventually brave it. I'm not sure about myself. First, there's the daunting chasm I anticipate will open in my life if he dies first. Secondly, a chorus of dearly-missed voices calls to *me* from these graves and would harrow me hard were I to attempt it without him.

I'd hear echoes from his parents, people who summoned the hopefulness to love me as a daughter-in-law (yet another!) despite their heartache over Tom's and my checkered marriage histories. There would surely be a word from Tom's aunt, whom I knew well and adored, now buried near his parents, who once exclaimed, "I think dying may turn out to be so interesting!" And then my wonderfully irreverent, sometimes aggravating brother-in-law, of whom I was very fond, would chime in with a hilarious joke. There would also be voices of those buried here that I never knew but still feel powerfully connected to, like the paternal grandfather mentioned above—a distinguished Methodist bishop-poet, subtly woven into Tom's and my relationship from its beginning. And that bishop's spunky mother, Nellie, whose spirit breathed through our green, rolling kisses so long ago, and after whom we planned to name a girl. For some, this cemetery might conjure only ghosts, but for me those ghosts have real substance, including a child no less real for never having been born.

The emotions surrounding loss and gain, grief and gratitude are complicated. Although these emotions are thought of as occurring separately, we often experience them simultaneously. When I spend time at this cemetery, for instance, I am usually flooded with gratitude tempered by sadness. And I never drive away without a backward glance of wistful thanks at having come again. A fragment of an old A.E. Housman poem my father once recited for me captures the convoluted yearning I experience on this ground, now hallowed by our many years of tending these graves:

Into my heart an air that kills
From yon far country blows:
What are those blue remembered hills,
What spires, what farms are those?

That is the land of lost content,
I see it shining plain,
The happy highways where I went
And cannot come again.

Sentimental? A bit. Outdated? Yes, if only because the words were written in the early twentieth century. But the poem also points to feelings that never go out of date, complex, intense emotions like cherishing. It isn't as simple as wishing that those we've loved and lost were alive again. If we are clear-headed, we know all too well how dead they are, and we have grieved their dying as fully as we've been able. And undeniably, our cherishing lives on in the traces of our grieving. That mixture of joy, sorrow, and acceptance strengthens our capacity to let go of those we love, as life itself bids us to do. The same mixture plaintively tints "those blue remembered hills."

In all this, emotional pain is predictable. We can't be present to a poignant moment without being pierced, or stung, which is the root of the word "poignant." In order to find meaning in a visit to the cemetery, I have to leave an emotional door ajar for the piercing "air that kills." If I fail to do that, it could rightly be said I never came at all. My body may have paid a visit, but my emotions will have been parked at the feet of the large marble angels at the entrance gate.

An experience of this grace-filled and penetrating poignancy happened to Tom on our trip to the cemetery a couple of years ago. It was not an experience he was seeking, nor one he was prepared for.

Tom will sometimes get up before me at our motel room in Vermont, leave quietly, and go find a cup of coffee at a gas station in town. On this particular morning he left the room well before dawn. Coffee in hand, he was inspired to drive to the cemetery. He told me later that he became aware of just how dark it was as the car bumped along the cemetery road and he saw the headlights rake the gravestones, shadows leaping high. After he brought the car to a stop next to where his family is clustered, he stepped out into the pitch black.

Nighttime and an early frost had set a chill in the air. This made him retrieve a towel from the back of the car to put under his butt as he planted himself on a gravestone. For some long minutes he sat there, "dropping down," as he later put it, into a place of silence and reflection. He closed his eyes. He felt a pervasive peace, he said, and a heightened quality in his attention.

As he sat on the stone, he suddenly sensed someone near him. There was no noise; he just felt a presence. He was tempted to open his eyes (this is, after all, a graveyard, and he can be spooked as much as the next guy), but did not. Before long, he felt *surrounded* by family members who had died—people he has loved his whole life, and whom he is confident love him. With his inner eye he could see them as clearly as when they'd been alive. No one spoke, but he experienced a powerful reassurance. Finally, he felt them blessing him. And then in an instant they were gone. He gradually opened his eyes. He was dumbfounded. It seemed as if an invisible bridge had been built which somehow joined the living to the dead. In the end, he was still sitting on the stone, only now he was saturated with astonishment, unable to move.

Tom didn't tell me about the experience until that afternoon. He needed to mull it over, to test his conviction that he hadn't concocted it. He knew he had not "invited" the encounter. The family members had appeared, unbidden. Perhaps most crucial for him, their affirmation overwhelmed him, as though it were being poured into him. He said the experience was not at all what he would have imagined or expected if his conscious mind had invented it, a peculiarity that validated its genuineness for him.

When he eventually did try to describe those mysterious moments to me, the telling caused him obvious pain. And while he talked, the tears he shed seemed to lack any guile. In relating some of the strongest emotions we human beings can feel—relief, longing, love, gladness, loss— his accounting felt devoid of a need to persuade or impress. At the same time, the experience had a forceful and ironic authority for him. It may have been as evanescent as an "air that kills," but it also felt as solid as the granite stone on which he'd been sitting.

A story like this usually gets rapidly dismissed; it's too alien to take seriously. Surrounded by dead family members who seem as real as your right hand? Please. Easily waved away.

Many of us, though, may hesitate to dismiss it. We're perhaps not likely to admit that hesitation to others, not if we hope to ward off raised eyebrows and accusations of wishful thinking. Some part of us, though, might lean toward mysteries beyond our mortal sight, asking questions of those mysteries. We are schooled to trust only what we experience with our five senses, but we may harbor a rebel who wonders whether those five senses always tell the whole truth.

That rebel lives in me, for sure. And while I might often tend to give a tale like this short shrift, it was my sober and powerfully reflective husband doing the talking. Rejecting it out of hand was too facile. Besides, I also knew certain things about his life that bore directly on the graveyard incident.

For instance, as a child Tom traveled with his family every summer from North Carolina to his grandfather's vacation home on a lake in New York State. Being at the lake house with a host of extended family members, especially his bishop grandfather, was ecstasy. During the school year in North Carolina, away from the larger family, Tom frequently felt real isolation, while time at the lake

was heaven. His grandfather was not an emotional intimate (few grandparents were, in the 1950s) but he was undeniably *there* for Tom: loving, available, compelling. And
due partly to these annual summer sojourns, the influence
of this grandfather on Tom's life has endured like carving
on Vermont marble.

Many decades later, then, when the inexplicable moments in the cemetery occurred, it's not hard to imagine
those childhood experiences reverberating up into the present. Tom's long-ago feeling of profound inclusion in the
cast of relatives, his gratitude, his overwhelming sense of
good fortune at knowing himself to be a member of his
particular family—all these were embedded in his psychic
"ground." It's as though some collective archetype, fully
alive inside him, became momentarily embodied. And
then vanished as quickly as it appeared. I'm not suggesting I understand this process, only that it seems plausible.

Did Tom's family "gather" at the graveyard in any
literal sense? Of course not. There was none of the tangible
solidity that we ascribe to what we call real. And yet this
event still strikes me as very real. Is it preposterous? Maybe. But preposterous doesn't necessarily cancel out real. It
depends on who's doing the defining. Many 21st century
Christians, for instance, would call the story of Jesus' res-
urrection *both* preposterous and real. There's no "explanation" for what happened that distant day on Calvary. And
yet it seems clear: *something* happened. More than 2,000
years of Christian believers attest to it—many, through the
ages, at the cost of their lives. And countless others are

convinced it was a day on which heaven (however we define it) and earth somehow came together, improbably and preposterously.

Gratitude often takes a long time to grow in us, to bear ripe fruit. If gratitude eventually permeates us, however, as it did Tom in this graveyard experience, it can produce a split second of heaven on earth. Under some conditions, a momentary merging of the earthly and celestial, the mortal and immortal, the human and divine—as appears to have transpired here—is perhaps not so odd at all. And not so easily dismissed.

Cemeteries are, in the end, far more than repositories for bones and ashes. They are sacred ground. They hold those we've loved and lost, those who cannot come again on Housman's earthly highway, happy or not. And they may become places where mystery and meaning and grace settle over us, oh so briefly, like a veil touched with the divine.

Whether or not something like this ever happens to Tom again, we will not be traveling to the cemetery in search of similar events. We *will* return there for the chance to dip back into the pool of gratitude that generated this strange experience and also flows from it. The quiet lanes that crisscross one particular Vermont graveyard are, as in all graveyards, lifelines to other times, other loves. And we will return to those lanes for as long as we can, until we can't.

Change of Heart

Some years back, in a book of mine called *Strenuous Blessings*, I wrote an essay entitled "Step." It was about how and why never having my own children created an echo of sadness that for decades felt as much a part of me as my right arm. The essay also explored certain emotional oddities of being a stepmother without being a mother.

I had once thought this faint despondency would be with me forever. But as I come to the end of my seventies, I realize it has now largely evaporated. In the face of decades-long loving relationships with my two stepdaughters and four grown grandchildren, that lingering sadness apparently didn't have a chance.

In a word, the original essay has been rendered untrue. Not completely—certain aspects of never having children of my own can still rattle me. But untrue in that the script in my heart has been re-written. Once upon a time, the interior voice I heard regarding children was a distant, plaintive song about the death of hopes and dreams. These days, as my own death draws closer, I mostly hear the high-spirited tunes from my large, loving tribe. That has been a sea change. To try and capture it, I've excerpted a few paragraphs from the original essay, identified them with italics, and then described how this change feels.

Having children—or not having them—does not define a woman or define who she can be. But having children, or not, does profoundly alter a woman's sense of herself and the way the world views her.

Consider a seemingly petty illustration: introductions in social situations. From the start, the girls have always winced when I named them as stepdaughters. They've resisted the "remove" of the term. And I have too; that remove inevitably gets thrust into any handshake. Yet omitting the "step" feels far worse to me because it seems fraudulent. If I'd already had children of my own when I joined up with my stepdaughters, I might well have sallied forth and introduced them as daughters. But, as it is, calling them daughters feels like a land grab for a country not mine.

A number of years ago, my stepdaughters and I (and their mother, Tom's first wife, with whom he and I have now long been friends) agreed that we would toss out the term "stepmother," which each of us, including Tom, disliked. I would become the girls' "mother-by-marriage" or mbm. We all loved the idea.

Much as I welcomed this move, there was an internal psychological gulf between calling myself by a new name and embracing its fullness. The name needed to evolve from a sweet hope, a clever sleight of hand, into something that felt genuine. Few of us, after all, treat "mother" as a light or easy concept, and being a mother-by-marriage, although less fraught, has its own distinct complexities. For me, the lived reality needed to come into focus over a long time, through an infinite number of moments. Those moments eventually formed themselves into a kind of shawl with *mother* woven far down in its threads, one I could wrap around me as I breathed a tentative *yes*.

Over the years, that *yes* gradually became more and more real for me. And yet, though I embraced being a mother-by-marriage, it was a private response. I felt like a non-mother publicly. And the divide between private and public emitted a subtle but steady drumbeat of self-doubt. The status of non-mother isn't often questioned outright; people aren't likely to be so crass. Non-motherhood, though, can sometimes generate penetrating inquiry, as in the following illustration.

Various arrows arc into the life of a stepmother without her own children. Such an arrow pierced me one morning, years ago, as I entered the vestibule of the church Tom and I were then serving in New York City. I was excited beyond measure: my younger stepdaughter had just given birth to a baby girl, the first grandchild, and I called out gleefully to an early gathering of parish-

ioners milling near the door, "Hey, I'm a grandmother!"
A woman in the group whom I didn't know well but
who knew enough about me to make this remark, said,
"How can you possibly be a grandmother if you've never
been a mother?"

Twenty-five years later, I can think of many sassy re-torts to the woman's question, but that morning I was stricken speechless. I don't remember how I responded. I do remember shrinking back into embarrassed dismay, as though I'd strayed into a party where I didn't belong. And the worst of it was, I secretly agreed with her. How could I possibly, indeed?

That kind of experience has everything to do with how we decide what's real and whose word we take for it besides our own. In an irony I prize, one of the people who advanced my understanding of this was the girls' mother, Barbara. Saying to me at some point, "You're as much a mother to the girls as I am," she created a brighter red-letter day for me than she knew. She then capped off the comment by urging that we get our picture taken together, which she suggested we give copies of to Tom and the girls for Mother's Day.

When Barbara and I arrived with framed prints of the picture to a Mother's Day lunch soon after, I grasped anew what counts for real. No, I hadn't birthed the babies. But the woman who *did* sat next to me at that lunch, with her arm firmly around my shoulder. The last time I saw the photo we took that now-distant day, it was on a table in a daughter's TV room, jumbled in with all the other pictures of the family. As though it had been there forever.

Then there was the morning, in a crowded first-grade classroom on Grandparents Visiting Day, when Tom and Barbara and I all took our seats on some very short chairs. He and she were both bursting with pride; I was still not sure of my place in the scheme of bursting things. After a time, each child was asked to name one favorite memory about a grandparent. As my granddaughter's turn came closer, I was conscious of holding a slight breath. Then she lisped through her missing front teeth, grinned wide, and whispered, "My favorite is my Nana's coffee cake."

There's a joyful internal eruption that can accompany grandparenting experiences, and I felt one then. What was happening? A brief blaze of silly pride, for sure. As well as laughter over Tom and Barbara ribbing me about my winning an emotional trophy that should rightly have gone to one of them, the actual grandparents. Looking back to that morning, though, I realize the joy came from my sense of *being an actual grandparent myself.* So much of what I'd felt as a stepmother hadn't ever seemed applicable to the grandchildren—all four of whom were by then little kids.

For me, that conviction of authenticity, of rightful place, has been a chief difference between being a stepmother and a grandmother. The world may still hold onto the "step"—one only needs to read obituaries to find multiple mention of step-grandchildren. But in my own grandmothering, no "step" has ever been even vaguely present. There's been no awkward distance, no apology, no specter of illegitimacy tracking me. In that initial instance of my grandmotherly delight in the church vestibule, the woman's words did make me hotly defensive. That defensiveness disappeared mighty fast, however, when it ran headlong into the love that each of the grandchildren turned out to give and take from me. And are still giving and taking now, decades later.

Social introductions prove the point. I can't imagine saying to someone, "I'd like you to meet my step grandson." Had I ever done so, any one of the four grandchildren, all young adults now, would surely have rounded on me afterwards, asking, "What was *that* supposed to mean, Nana?" A good question.

After many years of contentedly understanding myself as a mother-by-marriage, I was surprised to recently discover an unfinished piece of emotional business. Heartache made things plain. It first involved one daughter, stricken with a lethal illness in midlife and fighting valiantly through to recovery. Then almost simultaneously the other daughter, also in midlife, was plunged into the turbulent waters of a divorce.

During those two upheavals, I realized I had formerly been harboring a tiny piece of stepmother's distance, a certain sliver of abstraction. But the suffering involved in these events wasn't visited on daughters-in-the-abstract; it descended on people I love fiercely, not theoretically. As I lived through their suffering with them, any lingering abstraction dissolved.

Fresh strong currents appeared in my feelings. My worries changed, as did my prayers. Both of these grown children now "inhabited" me in a new way. When I woke up in the mornings, I felt their difficulties keenly; their fateful decisions ran through my own psyche. And eventually I understood: this is the country of mothers and children. Daughters were no longer always someone else's, they were also mine.

The process came full circle when Tom and I each went through difficult medical challenges recently, he with an illness and me with debilitating back trouble. We suddenly felt old. We knew our capacity to care for ourselves was temporarily eclipsed, that we couldn't stay alone on the island. We moved in with one daughter, in Portland, and both daughters cared for us until we recovered. Again, it was clear. The intimate attentiveness this entailed was the preserve of parents and children. The stepmother had finally picked up her skirts and left for another country. I'm not saying I couldn't conjure her—just that she became irrelevant.

Despite certain cultural assumptions, stepmothering doesn't "fix" things for the woman without children of her own. There's a straightforward reason. Just as a woman with children can never "un-know" the realness

of them, so the woman without *children can't ever*
"know" herself into a realness that doesn't exist for her.
Once a woman has children, she automatically moves in-
to a world that the childless woman, whether she's a
stepmother or not, can't inhabit.

That paragraph is still true. And it isn't. The reality is
much more complicated.

In the literal sense, there is no cure for not having
one's own biological children. And yet, as I said in the
original essay, ask an adoptive mother who's been at it for
years what her opinion on this subject is. Only a hardcore
literalist would remain unconvinced.

For any stepmother fortunate enough to be caught in
the arms of loving children and grandchildren, there's a
larger healing at work. It transcends birth lines, erases lit-
eralisms of all sorts. Mysterious, elusive, and as real as a
knock-kneed, lisping first grader, this healing is all that
counts in the end.

Childless is indeed a bona fide state of being. But it can
also become a profound contradiction in terms, as it has
for me. I have children all right, they just weren't born to
me. Does that shawl with *mother* woven into it, the one I
put on so long ago, have holes in it? It sure does. When I
think of it, I'll ask the kids and grandkids whether those
holes matter.

Belonging

It's wonderful to grow old living in the place you loved most as a child.

It's painful to grow old living in the place you loved most as a child.

Spending all my girlhood summers on a Maine island taught me a joyful early irony: fixed geographical boundaries can create enormous freedom.

As long as you could swim and were adept at finding a path through the woods, wisdom back then said you would be fine. On a slice of rock and spruce a half mile wide and less than five miles long almost everyone knew your family, and chances were if you got into a scrape somebody would deliver you home by supper. Meanwhile, day in and day out, once the household tasks were finished, you were gloriously free. Free to play at whatever you chose, to bike a continent away to the other end of the island, to lie in the long grass doing nothing weightier than watch the high clouds passing.

This is a description of intense privilege—of being born to a woman who fetched up on the island thanks to a close friend with a family house here. Eventually she and my father, once grace returned him home after World War II, bought a small cottage and filled it with my two sisters and me. It's the privilege of growing up during an era so old-fashioned that until my mother moved the hands on the chiming clock in our island kitchen and tapped the brass pendulum to swing again, summer had not yet begun.

At least this is how she put it to my young self. I loved to watch her move that pendulum upon our annual June arrival, loved the promise of the coming three months shimmering in front of me like a field of shiny coins. Though I knew our Labor Day departure would bring me anguish, I felt rich when the clock began ticking in June. As did my mother, evidenced by her big grin. She is now long gone, but her implied message is as clear to me in my late seventies as it was then: *Cherish this time and place you've landed, Little Miss. Be grateful, because you are one lucky child.*

How right she was. And among all the gifts given by those consecutive summers none proved dearer to me than a sense of belonging. Together with wind and sky and salty expeditions, it got spliced into my spirit while I wasn't looking, years before I grasped the strength of the splice.

That strength isn't the hardness of iron or wood. It's more like the delicate, durable baskets we bought from the Penobscot families who came to camp on the island for a few days every year. These were sweet-grass baskets, well known to hold a trace of their sunny scent for decades. My grandmother and then my mother prized a certain one for sewing; as its current owner, I occasionally sniff it to see whether the scent still remains. It does.

There is much about life on the island that continues to sustain a strong feeling in me of stability and belonging. Many relationships, some casual, some deep, have been in place since childhood. Newer relationships, differently enduring, have developed since Tom and I became year-round residents twenty-five years ago. And then there are people once known only tangentially who have late in life become sources of great affection and delight. All these connections are rooted in the experiences—some very subtle—that come from multiple years of sharing this particular water-bound bit of territory.

There are also many natural marks of constancy. Wild blueberries grow in the same spots; a setting sun casts the same gold-rose glow, winter and summer, over long fields. And if I follow a certain path to the shore, in the right month, at the right tide, I'll find a stand of beach heather growing where it always has, to the left of some mossy rocks.

When I was young, the feeling of belonging was as dependable as the chime from our kitchen clock. Everything about life on the island back then seemed to amplify this regularity. It shone out of multiple familiar faces as they came into focus for yet another season. It rang from the square dances held every Saturday night at the antiquated hotel, as people of all ages were drawn in droves to the light and music spilling from the building. And I felt it in spades, year after year, when I got chucked under the chin by a certain lobsterman, relishing his mock surprise at my growing up.

Belonging—and the longing in both the word and the emotion—is a feeling so complex in its layers of people and place, of time present and past, that it defies capture. Yet the fact of it, the truth of it, is as close as our breathing. When we say I belong in *this* house, in *these* arms, in *this* church, we know what we mean. We feel at home, secure, someone would notice if we were missing. Once upon a time, I knew as surely as my first name was Mary that I *belonged* at that square dance every Saturday night and would have fought my parents to a draw if they'd tried to keep me away. But if I'd been asked to "describe" my impatience to bolt from our family's pre-dance dinner table? Any explanation would have been swallowed by my fever to yes, please, now, be *gone*...released at last into the experience itself.

Just as we know in our bones what belonging is, though, we also know when the sensation is missing. Or when it begins to fade. In regard to life in a particular place, the feeling of belonging may not actually disappear, but it can begin to get elbowed out. Confidence in it might still be strong, but it can *start to co-exist with its own undo-*

ing.

To give an example: living on the island involves a ride on one of two ferries. One ferry is regularly chosen not just because the trip is short, but because it delivers a lot of social interaction. For years too numerous to count, people riding this boat on any given trip knew each other. All the passengers were neighbors, friends, acquaintances you were glad to see, and a few you maybe weren't. Strangers were a rarity.

In recent years, change has exerted its forceful hand over that portrait. Especially during the summer. Like many communities along the coast of Maine, we've become a seasonal destination for day trippers, transient wedding guests, bicycle riders by the battalion. Starting in late May, ferry trips are thronged with strangers. And a note, spoken or not, soon arises from the regular passengers like a dissonant drumbeat: who *are* all these people?

To be fair, except for actual visitors, many of the "strangers" are likely to be the children and grandchildren of friends with whom we once played hide-and-go-seek. These offspring have grown up and bought or inherited houses on the island. It's hardly their fault if they're not easy to recognize. Surely my own extended family, altered like others through divorce and re-marriage, generates a similar alienation for ferry passengers who may know Tom and me but don't know the people attached to us. In other words, plenty of the so-called strangers belong on the boat as much as any of the rest of us.

The problem is: it doesn't feel that way. From the

long-time resident's end of the telescope, it feels like an invasion. It's as though something deeply familiar and trustworthy is being upended. And no matter who rolls in on this high tide of the unfamiliar—even if it's a boatload of descendants—a steady influx of those-who-seem-like-strangers dilutes a former feeling of stability.

It's true that many old social customs remain woven into the fabric of island life. Like innumerable New England villages, we are a place of friendliness, unshowy kindness, and generosity. We take food to families stricken by illness or death. We wave to passing cars on the road whether we know the other driver or not, an island tradition for generations. We continue to leave keys in unlocked cars. And a lost child will surely still get returned to the right house in time for supper.

All these community norms reinforce belonging, strengthen a certain trust. Yet forces now exist that also erode those same norms, forces rooted in unfamiliarity. The rise in newcomers means many on the island don't know each other anymore. It isn't that everyone knew each other previously in some deep intimate sense, but rather that everyone was known *to* one another. Including the recluses. In a small community, such knowing counts for a great deal, even if what it counts for is mostly indefinable.

Since strangers have become a commonplace on the island, particularly in the summertime, that earlier knowing has shifted. When unfamiliar people are roaming around, an atypical caution enters the picture. Doors start to quietly lock; mystery prompts questions. And over time, as the unfamiliar drips steadily onto the familiar, it seeps down through the complexities of belonging. At least it does for me. Again, *the belonging doesn't vanish.* But caution, guardedness—all the subtle disruptions that accompany what's unknown—are ingredients that dilute belonging's former strength.

Various other shifts in community life have taken place over the past couple of decades. Taken all together, these changes can feed a curious sensation that the island has turned into another place. It hasn't, but it sometimes *seems* as though it has. Are the roads and shoreline the same? Yes. Do boats ride at their anchors as always? Yes. Does the dense, timeless smell of the fog persist, like the inside of those sweet-grass baskets? Yes.

Unvarying hallmarks like these, though, can make changes more noticeable. It's part of having a long lens, something irrelevant to a newcomer. Change is almost bound to feel disturbing if we grow old where the music of childhood still drifts through the trees. Similarly, memories unearthed from long-familiar ground may surface with pangs.

For instance, standing on the ferry dock not long ago, returning in the late afternoon from a grocery trip to the mainland, I heard two young women who'd been on the boat with me calling animatedly to each other as they slung shopping bags into their cars. I didn't know their names, but their vitality didn't need a name. In planning a future supper party, they radiated the energy and bustle of twenty-somethings and appeared undaunted by the stiff

October wind and falling light.

Meanwhile, in my late-seventies, loading my own grocery bags, I couldn't have entertained a plan of any description, let alone yelled it across a blustery dock. Depleted from the mainland trip, all I could manage was to stow my own gear in the car, heave my grateful body into the front seat, and head for home. Even so, their exhilarated words on the wind coursed through my veins with bittersweet force. I wanted to call out to them, *it wasn't so long ago that I was you, ladies, with your verve and kick*...but indeed, it was a very long time ago.

If we are lucky, if we are graced, we get to live into the joys of old age. And if we are especially lucky, we live them in a place deeply, wonderfully familiar. At the same time, if that place is alive and growing, it will change, sometimes radically, generating its rightful, new, insistent demands. Almost by definition, what might then feel fresh and grand to a newcomer may feel woefully out of sync—and oddly painful—to the child now grown old.

The joys of old age can also be muted by heightened awareness of time passing. The sound of sand running through the hourglass gets louder, no matter where we end our days. When death casts its shadow, though, over the ground where our growing up was once sky-blue forever, it carries a particular poignancy. The sense of belonging to something solid can merge with a sense of that solidity dissolving. Eventually, dissolution starts to win the match.

As long as we are young, this awareness of time rolling forward has only a light grip on us; death is usually no more substantial than a butterfly on the wing. And barring the death of someone close to us, its reality will probably remain insubstantial for a long time.

Then the evidence starts to mount. Some beloved figure dies, and death is no longer an abstraction. That happened for me in my early thirties, the morning we set my father's ashes down into a snowy rough-cut hole in the island cemetery. From then on, I began to understand how death's thievery erodes a sense of belonging, as it steals the people who make that belonging real and rich. This realization was amplified for me again, one day in the cemetery, as I passed by the gravestone of the chin-chucking lobsterman of my early summers. I stopped there in the warm sun by his grassy plot, recalling his rough hand against my young face. It was wonderful—and it was painful—to reflect on the affection bestowed on me years before I could feel the weight of its loss.

Death's thieving had long been evident to me when my oldest island friend died a few years ago, in a bitter cold November. But it took on further meaning then. From our youngest days, she was the person I couldn't wait to see when we arrived in June, the one I most hated to leave as the clock edged toward another Labor Day. Between those two markers, summer after summer, we were together almost constantly. And even though she moved from the island to the mainland many years ago, she never moved out of my spirit.

When I was asked to speak at her funeral at the island

church, I wasn't sure I'd be able to pull it off. But I badly wanted to. We share those sky-blue days, after all, with a very small number of people. I partly quavered at the prospect of speaking because I knew that, in sending her on her way, a crucial page from my own book of belonging was going with her. I also knew she would have relished the obvious joke: that soon enough my own name would be carved into a piece of slate, planted not far from hers. To end up a stone's throw apart, waving across the cemetery's ancient forget-me-nots, made a certain laughable sense, even as it made me tremble to try to express why it all mattered.

As I stood up at the church lectern, however, and felt penetrating sadness over her death, gratitude for her life strengthened my knees. Not just gratitude for her, but for the place that had formed us both and bound us together for so long with its unwritten, indelible rules. Gratitude that she, shy and eager, welcomed me back every summer; that she was the one who first took me, with great glee, to the Penobscot in their tents; that she biked with me and swam with me and led us through the woods pretending to be fearless Micmac maidens. And gratitude that she was the one who much later understood deep down what it might be like, even though we talked about it very little, for me to have no babies when she had six.

Lament may rise in our throats, but gratitude gets the last word. A faded sense of belonging can be hard to embrace, and yet I suspect that the fade is exactly what is supposed to happen when our life is on the home stretch, especially if it plays out on beloved turf. Each of us is destined to lose our own field of belonging. If it were not so, we would be living something other than real life and its bracing terms—with death as the built-in disappearing act. In my heart the Micmac maid might run forever through the island underbrush, but in truth her traces fly upward and disappear like sparks from a driftwood fire on a dark night. Which means that all belonging is fleeting from the very start, our lives both green *and* dying in the same wonderful flash.

Please, Not Too Close

One of the most distressing features of the coronavirus era, at its height, was the ban on touching people other than those we were intimately and regularly connected to.

This prohibition carried a particular challenge for those of us in our seventies, eighties, and beyond. We were keenly aware that, whether we contracted the virus or not, the end of our days was within hailing distance. Having to avoid physical closeness with those we cared about was painful, knowing all closeness would be gone for good soon enough. At the same time, the toll of illness and death the virus took among older people was so high that belly-aching about the lack of actual touch bordered on a whine. Images of people marooned in nursing homes or hospitals, reduced to "touching" those they loved only through glass doors and windows, shut complaint down fast from those of us not marooned. And still, it was hard to go without the contact.

I got a dose of this when the virus was just a few

months old, as I walked out onto our screened-in porch one summer morning and found one of our twenty-five-year old granddaughters talking to Tom. I knew her plan had been to catch a late boat out to the island that day; she'd arrived much earlier. Calling out her name in surprised pleasure, I automatically went forward to give her a hug. Until Tom protested. Firmly. He reminded me to pull away, to back up.

He was right. But it felt all wrong. True: we didn't know where she had been and with whom. *But this was one of our beloved grandchildren.* Normally, it would not have occurred to me to care where she had been. But I was being served notice—again—that I needed to care. Tom had cut me a slice of the loaf, slathered with caution, that was now our daily bread. I backed away from her and ate it, ruminating, yet again, on how this highly infectious disease had fused spontaneous desire with restraint.

A similar experience happened to a friend of mine named Kate. Long before the virus descended, she and her husband, both in their seventies, had become American mainstays for a young refugee couple who settled in Portland. Great affection developed among the four of them. A son was born to the family after they arrived in the United States; three years in, Kate doted on the boy and he on her.

When Kate and her husband, after weeks of no contact, stopped by this family's house one day, the virus had started to become a fact of life. But masks and safe-distance practices were not yet automatic. As the child spied their car pulling into the driveway, he hit the ground running, bolting across the yard to make his usual leap into what he was sure would be Kate's open arms. She knelt low to catch him, and then abruptly realized her mistake. She stood up fast, folded her arms into her chest, and when he landed at her feet touched him lightly on the top of his head. She described it later as a weak, contradictory gesture, divorced from her true impulse. The grownups flapped around trying to fix the moment with explanations for the mystified child, but to no avail—the deflating arrow had hit its mark.

Kate said something collapsed inside her too when she saw the disappointment on the boy's face. She knew she'd had no choice: she's an elderly, recent cancer survivor, he's an active toddler with a life full of chance encounters. But having chosen the "right" response, she experienced a deeply unpleasant aftertaste—the by-now-familiar flavor of eagerness, thwarted.

I think, also, about some grandparents experiencing that same flavor when they learned of a ban on close contact with their young grandson. Acutely conscious of their dwindling years, they pressed the hesitant new parents to lift the ban. The grandparents won the tussle, but the victory produced a certain chafe.

All this awkwardness the virus raised around physical closeness was borne in on me when Tom and I were invited to attend an August wedding on the island. Only twenty guests would be there; we'd known most of them for decades. I had a particular tie to the bride. She and I shared childhood summers on the island and her re-marriage exerted a strong pull to attend the wedding.

But Tom and I were both reluctant to go. Although we would be outdoors, and plans were in place about seating, distancing, and serving of food, we were still wary. After months of near-total isolation as a couple, the thought of *any* gathering felt uncomfortable. Events we once viewed as easygoing were now hedged with anxiety. And despite the agreed-upon restrictions, our confidence in those was weak. Indeed, we hadn't been at the party for long before guests began drifting over the presumptive six-foot divides, voicing sheepish apology as if they had broken through yellow crime-scene tapes. Eventually, in all sorts of settings, moments like these spawned a certain absurd pandemic drama, a kind of exaggerated self-consciousness over behaviors reluctantly adopted.

As it got more routine to venture out again into the world, attitudes toward maintaining distance came into focus. Some people were ultra-vigilant, almost paranoid, and would express fear or move away when another person came too close. Others were almost blasé and seemed only dimly committed to keeping a long arm's length. And then there were the lapses common to most of us: forgetting the rules, remembering, forgetting again—a pattern evident in constant return trips to the car for a mask left behind.

No matter where a person fetched up on the attitude scale regarding social distancing, the new awkwardness about physical closeness permeated every social gathering. Compelled to be acutely mindful of the need for separation from each other meant that, emotionally, *the focus was always in the wrong place*. Even though it was the right place. Instead of relating naturally to one another, though, we were mentally measuring space, alert to the potential need to strap on a mask. Or ask someone to back up from us. These dance steps, rarely seen in any previous social setting, lent new meaning to the definition of awkward.

This confusion around how and where to focus may partly explain why some people rebelled against the new practices. Since physical restraint had been *dictated*, it was judged questionable, even rejected outright. To others, the imposition of strict rules was a relief; ignoring the rules felt willful. Eventually the gap between those points of view filled up with emotional frustration. People tended to congregate with those they felt agreed with them on the issue of risk, and while that didn't eliminate the edginess, it brokered the tension somewhat.

Awkwardness also expanded into related behaviors. In all but our intimate relationships, we had to stifle natural expressions of emotion. This led to foolish-feeling substitute gestures like mock embraces and elbow bumping. While eminently sensible, those gestures were in turn usually accompanied by lopsided grins acknowledging the poverty of the substitutes, all of which became part of the virus-generated language of disembodied yearning and regret.

Compared to the death toll from the virus, concern with these odd psychological costs feels unimportant, especially among the elderly. Most older people who survived the virus counted themselves lucky to be alive; awkward behaviors were a minor matter. Besides, those of *any* age could imagine the peculiarities were only temporary, that before long we would be restored to our natural selves.

And perhaps we will. But there's a quiet hunch that some behaviors could end up forever changed. Yes, the pall cast by the virus will surely lift to some extent. But we may also find ourselves afflicted with an enduring hesitancy, living in a world where physical closeness gets permanently re-defined.

This could apply to all sorts of practices some of us take for granted. Take passing the sign of peace in churches, for instance, when people extend a hand or a hug or occasionally even a kiss to someone nearby in a pew. Introducing hesitation to that ritual might be a welcome change for some! But the larger point holds. For those of us inclined to express ourselves freely with others not intimately connected to us, we may never again feel a former freedom. Even when the virus has seemingly been conquered, we will not know where another person has been, or with whom. And rather than take a chance, or just because the whole subject is too thorny, we may well opt to stick with the mock embraces and apologetic shrugs. It's likewise possible to imagine how the extension of a handshake, once so routine, could disappear into yesterday and never be heard from again.

There is a general view that if we can just avoid the virus altogether, or at least escape its worst ravages, the black cloud will depart and leave us essentially un-changed. Now, a few years in, it seems plausible that our behaviors and the complex emotional factors binding them together may be profoundly altered. The virus has en-snared us all in its web, and the protective actions we've adopted could be much harder to reverse than we think. Not because we'll be in literal danger, but because we'll continue to be haunted by the threat of that danger. And the older we are, the more haunted we are perhaps going to feel.

No matter what, our once-automatic instincts about distance and closeness will probably remain conflicted. A kind of instinct, after all, usually prompts the routine handshake or hug. We might wish we *could* act with open-heartedness, but we may opt to curb that openness as deci-sively after the pandemic as during it. Will I throw a garland of kisses around the neck of another childhood friend, bravely re-marrying at a ripe old age? Unlikely. Will my friend Kate feel free to once again scoop up that child flying toward her on his newly-minted American feet? Perhaps not. Or not anytime soon.

If the virus does abate for real, the *last* thing we will want is ongoing consciousness of its emotional legacy. And yet, virus-generated wariness could stick to us as stubbornly as our own shadows. The image of those yearn-ing hands pressed against the glass may remain— reminding us of the peril we once risked through close contact, and the price we've paid for the loss of it.

A Particular Loneliness

How difficult it is to talk with a person who is dying...about dying. No, not just difficult. Almost impossible. Many of us may have a powerful urge to speak, but there's an equally strong urge to clam up. The subject is too big, too scary; we hardly know where to begin.

I'm not referring to the death of an intimate, like a spouse. In those heart-rending situations, when we're granted enough time, most of us will stumble through our agony and find some words—if not the exact ones we hoped for. I'm talking more about dying friends, acquaintances, relatives; people we may be very fond of and perhaps haven't seen recently. Faced with their death, trying to articulate our emotions can feel overwhelming.

It's complicated. Adoring helpers, though ready to meet all manner of needs, are not necessarily eager to listen to a dying person's thoughts and feelings. And not all those staring at imminent death *want* to speak of it; they can be as pot-bound as everyone else. They also may be too ill to summon enough energy to talk. Or they worry about making others feel bad if they reveal themselves. Whatever the reason, meaningful conversation can elude the one doing the dying, and can lead to a large dose of loneliness for them.

Tom and I recently had an experience of this yes-let's talk-about-it-no-let's-not complexity. We went to visit some friends, aware that the man of the couple did not have long to live. A dread disease had nailed him; it was now exacting an ever-greater toll in breath, energy, and strength.

For a while the four of us yielded to small talk. Tom and I didn't suggest otherwise. This couple were well aware that, when we were employed as clergy, we'd had lots of end-of-life conversations. But these were friends. We didn't want to trespass on ground where we hadn't been invited.

An invitation wasn't long in coming. After we explored concerns related to his medical care, the man indicated he wanted to stop skirting the subject of his dying. He said he had recently been challenged by his son, himself eager for direct talk. Our friend then told us he had met with a doctor from the organization Death with Dignity. In concert with the doctor, he had decided, when the time came, to end his own life.

It was a startling admission. As people who are ourselves approaching eighty, we had thought and talked about what we might do if faced with an intractable, steadily worsening illness.

Beyond his admitted intention, though, we were far more taken aback by the energy that surged through this extremely ill man after he told us his plans. Up until then, fettered by chat, he had been reserved, faintly depressed. Now he was animated. His speaking was buoyant, his face alight with his familiar laugh.

Though there are many potential explanations for such zest, common to them all is a single truth we could see writ large: his high-spiritedness grew like a sunflower out of the opportunity to talk. He was eager for others to engage the fact of his dying—which was, after all, his own central preoccupation. He wanted company! He wanted to talk with friends, well-wishers, fellow travelers. The animation came from relief at being able to discuss what was happening to him and briefly stop feeling like an outcast from the human family.

He said he didn't need to be discussing his death non-stop, but he hoped for the reality of it to become normalized, out in the open. In other words, he wanted what we so often fail to provide in the face of death: real talk. He made it clear that unless his impending death was at least tacitly part of a conversation, there was no genuine place for him *in* the conversation. And such exclusion, even if unintended, was a surefire prescription for loneliness.

As things unfolded from there, I understood again the power of *talk that confronts the reality being experienced*. Even when—perhaps especially when—that reality is death. Discussion of death is raw. It can pierce; it may prompt lots of tears. It will bring us close to the quick. But when someone says he wants companions as he approaches his death, the "quick" is exactly the point.

The value of frank conversation snapped further into focus when our friend described a project he had embarked on with his daughter. She is a professional writer, accustomed to tackling gritty material; this was a different kind of gritty. She and her father had agreed to record him talking about his life and his coming death, and she would eventually transcribe his words. They weren't sure what would happen with the finished writing. It didn't matter. What mattered was the emotional intimacy their collaboration delivered. Traveling to depths that fathers and daughters might often avoid had, by his account, given him a big jolt of new life—plenty of quick, as it were. And that was the region he hoped to inhabit to the end, in the close company of those he loved.

People on the verge of death need to experience the emotional willingness this daughter showed. Whether or not they can embrace it, they need the offer of it. When others shy away, it just makes the dying person hesitant to share his feelings or even admit to a knotty hesitation. At least in America, we've all grown up in the same death-averse culture. Avoiding the subject of death, though, only works as long as death remains at a remove. When death draws near, denial collapses. For all of us. And if the dying person can't find real companions and real talk, loneliness will seep into the empty spaces.

The question is whether we, the currently hale and upright, have the heart to discern a dying person's hunger for connection and join ourselves to it. Fortunately, doing so is not simply an exercise in altruism. Besides offering potent help, engagement like this also enriches and broadens our own lives. Enormously.

For starters, when we are genuinely attentive to someone who's dying, we will reap the rewards of listening more fully than we normally do. Our listening will be deepened to a degree we perhaps thought impossible and, if we are fortunate, our emotional responsiveness will follow suit.

Listening in this enlarged way, we're also likely to experience a type of quiet that is other than a zone of confused retreat. It can be a profoundly resonant quiet—echoing the monk, Thomas Merton, who long ago pointed out that God's first language is silence. Attentive silence, along with the spaciousness that emerges from it, are gifts to anyone who needs to be heard. And when we have been instrumental in creating that space, we receive a powerful parallel blessing.

The counterpoint of silence and reflective talk can also result in a whole other order of conversation. If someone has made it clear they want to focus on their impending death, the discussion is apt to be blunt and purposeful. It's unlikely to be punctuated by anxious rambling, or nervous laughter, or trivialities. One of the wonders of talking with a dying person is the lack of time for trivialities. They, after all, are nearly out of time.

Perhaps most importantly, conversations with someone who's dying can lead us into a new kind of patience.

That's because those conversations will bring us close to someone's suffering and illuminate the direct connection between suffering and patience.

Someone facing death may not be in literal pain, but they are suffering the imminent loss of everything they love. When we allow ourselves to absorb the weight of that loss, our appreciation for the bravery of the human spirit will grow. As will our patience. Seeing someone's life ebb away humbles us, sparks our empathy, and inspires our patience, in the fullest sense of that word. It's no accident that the words "patience" and "suffering" share a linguistic root—rightly understood, they find their meaning in one another.

As we got ready to leave our friend and his wife, their mood was a mix of joy, sorrow, uplift and tears, a match for our own. We didn't know whether we would see him again, but it somehow wasn't the point. In our conversation the four of us had joined hands and crossed the chasm between the still-living and the close-to-dying. Briefly and imperfectly, but we'd crossed it—putting a certain loneliness to flight for all of us.

Forgive Us Our Trespasses

The older I get, the more I crave the relief that comes from admitting a trespass and being forgiven. Of course, like lots of people, I fear getting shut out of someone's affection if I'm found in the wrong. At least with Tom, though, the opposite almost always happens. He's no saint, but acknowledgment of fault usually opens his heart. As soon as I admit my role in a squabble, out comes his empathetic smile and some forgiving word. There's no hint of shaming, or self-congratulation from him about being right— just forgiveness, and its partner: freedom.

Expectation of that charity isn't automatic for me. As a child I was prone to stray well beyond the borders of Naughty, which meant shame appeared regularly on my plate. In those days, shaming children was not viewed as negatively as it is today. It was also common practice back then for parents to withhold forgiveness in the interests of moral instruction. In any era, however, whenever shame persists in someone's psyche, it has formidable staying power. The following story, told to me by someone at our church, illustrates this.

One weekday morning, two employees showed up for work at the church to find an object dangling from the front door handle, awkwardly tied on with a thick rubber band. It was a brass candlestick from the altar, with a note attached: *I stole this from the church in 1971. A lifetime of regret has no cure. I was 12. Sincerely, Robert*

1971. Doing the math, Robert was now in his sixties. Perhaps he was cleaning out a house and had unexpectedly come across the candlestick, buried for a long time. Perhaps. Since buried doesn't mean forgotten, it's more likely that he knew exactly where it was. Maybe he "always meant" to return it; maybe he'd often considered ways to slip into the church parking lot under cover of night and unload the pirated item. Whatever his struggle, it took him more than 50 years to act. While carrying this burden for half a century feels excessive, most of us have our own stories of "always meant to" and never following through. Few people are complete strangers to Robert's regret. There is often some heaviness, however small, that we would love to cast off and be forgiven for.

We're not usually quick, however, to do that casting off—and definitely not at twelve years old. We might like to imagine young Robert summoning his courage to return to the church the next day, hoping whoever he encountered would be kind. But it's a naïve thought. He'd be more likely to fear a verbal trouncing, first from some church authority and then from a newly-notified parent.

It's hard to overstate the mental traps we create for ourselves in regard to forgiveness. Robert's words, *a lifetime of regret has no cure*, may sound overwrought. But down where we all live, where shame and relief are joined, his sad little note hits the emotional nail on the head. It was predictable that all Robert could do in the end was tie the candlestick on the door and vanish. He couldn't trust, even so many decades later, that compassion, or mercy—or a hearty laugh—might well be extended if he showed up with the booty in his hand and apology in his heart.

We assume that it's easy to become a forgiving person. But it isn't. And it can be a monumentally difficult capacity to develop if we haven't been helped to name our own misdeeds and felt genuinely forgiven for them.

Think how many of us, as adults, are unskilled at pursuing creative solutions to conflict. Whether it's a disagreement with a co-worker, a spat with a spouse, or an unpleasant misunderstanding with a neighbor, we often sidestep the quickest path out of the trouble. Untangling the knot that conflict produces is usually obvious. Irritatingly obvious. Almost always, the faster we admit our own responsibility in the situation, the sooner the knot will ease, the sooner forgiveness will release its singular balm.

The economy of forgiveness, though, depends on our coming clean to the other party and then doing whatever it takes to work through the trouble. If Robert *had* been able back then to screw up his courage and return to the church, with luck and a dollop of grace he might have encountered a wise soul. This person, if judicious as well as wise, would have known that forgiveness contains an infinitely more beneficial lesson than shaming. After a firm but temperate scolding, and before contacting his parents, the boy could have been granted the forgiveness that by right was his. As it was, unable to fess up to anyone, he got sealed into the amber of self-reproach.

A monk I know once remarked that we ought to consider cultivating practices in life that will wear well in eternity. Indeed, and we don't have to be in eternity's neighborhood to practice his insight. The younger we are when we understand this, the better off we'll be.

Just as I didn't realize until a later age, though, how much I yearned for the freedom of being forgiven, I also hadn't completely grasped the need to *become* more forgiving—even of those we may find it most difficult to forgive. And to do this not just for the other person's sake, but for our own. When we forgive others, we become an equal, if not greater, beneficiary. Whatever our forgiveness may do for someone else, our own spirit expands.

The same applies to many related actions. If we offer compassion, our storehouse of compassion will grow. So too with empathy, or mercy, or openheartedness. We are always enlarged when we extend these charitable traits to others, provided, that is, we don't get mired in self-congratulation over our own benevolence.

We know the truth of this through behaviors that cause our souls to shrink. Can any of us be unfamiliar with those? Think of getting smug satisfaction out of someone else's flaws. Or giving our judgmentalism the upper hand just when it ought to be reined in. Or insisting on being right, even in matters of little importance. All of these trespasses have been mine, as well as many more troublesome ones. If indulged, they not only alienate others but diminish us spiritually.

Which means such behaviors also harden our hearts. Whenever we're bogged down in judgement of another, however secretly, we're likely to be patting our own backs all the way to an imagined moment of reckoning—always for the other person. In that sense, self-congratulation feeds internal hardness and rigidity, while charity or empathy make us permeable and expansive. Being able to astutely judge various life experiences isn't the issue; judgmentalism is.

While forgiveness as a spiritual challenge signifies at any age, it looms larger at the end of our lives. Our capacity to become a fully forgiving human being is deeply consequential for those we love and are leaving behind. Whatever needs to be forgiven between us while we're both on the same side of the grass ought to happen in full—for everyone's liberation.

But we need help in this. At least I do. And the older I get, the more help I need. The task of keeping smallness of spirit at bay always takes some doing. When I heard that one of the women who found the candlestick on the door intended to polish off the 50 plus years of tarnish and return it to the altar, I wished I'd been a clergyperson working at that church. I would have been sorely tempted to swipe the item back, leave its tarnish intact, and install it on my office desk. When reminding myself or another person about our lifelong imperative to get spiritually bigger not smaller, that candlestick could have come in mighty handy.

Wild Geese Going Over

By the time we reach old age, the kind of amazement we felt in childhood has long since disappeared. And the way we experience being amazed has grown much more complex.

When we're children, amazement can engulf us. Sunk into self-forgetfulness, we focus intensely, we block interference. The interplay between our dreams and schemes can stop time.

This all changes with adulthood. Time not only doesn't stop, but the older we get the more it plunges forward at breakneck speed. And though we may be able to summon a ferocious degree of focus as adults, we are rarely self-forgetful in the sense that children are. We've lived too long and know too much to forget either ourselves or our surroundings; the expectation that we'll relinquish self-focus is almost built into the word "adult".

As we grow older, we also get tempered by disappointment, perhaps deep sorrow, and by the inevitable wear and tear of life, all of which can diminish our capacity for amazement. We usually adjust to this decline without much visible fuss. When we are grown up, however, it matters—for us and those we love—whether we are still able to summon amazement ourselves or participate in the amazement of others, particularly that of children.

I remember a long-ago summer afternoon on the island when my best friend and I, both seven or eight years old at the time, found mussels clinging to a pile of rocks on the beach. Prying a few open, we were awestruck by the tiny pearl we found inside each shell. We looked at each other. There were *hundreds* of mussels, probably *thousands.* Clutching some specimens, we flew home to show my friend's mother: Pearls! Galore! We were rich!

With a couple of deft yet gentle strokes, she gave us a simple version of how "pearls" get formed inside mussel shells. All my life I've been able to recall the participatory spirit of her response—setting us straight, but not bruising our overheated wonder. Do I think now that she laughed at us behind our backs? I am confident she did not. At least not derisively. If she had, I would have seen it in her eyes and heard it in her voice. As it is, whenever I find one of those pearls in a mussel, I'm still not sure it isn't worth *something…*

Children's amazement is tied to their as-yet limited life spans. For adults, amazement has radically different sources. It arises out of living through multiple experiences that were harsh, wonderful, and all the ambiguous combinations in between.

In a phrase coined during his own later life, the poet Stanley Kunitz named our awareness of these varied experiences as "living in the layers." By the time we reach old age, the layers contain countless leaves of rich memory and meaning, laid down over many years. Much trouble is lodged there, alongside great gladness, shattered dreams, and dreams gloriously realized. These compacted and highly personal experiences can be stirred, will be stirred, by events in the present, which may then prompt our amazement.

There are of course other kinds of amazement not based on former experience, such as what happens to us when we travel in another country for the first time. Or, say, witness an astronaut's rocket lifting off. But in the case of the rocket, the very lack of "layers" inside us is the point. The technical wizardry of that achievement may be intense, and yet it is unlikely to strike a deep chord of personal meaning. The astonishment evoked tends to be fleeting and superficial, a fact reflected in our current overuse of the word "awesome," which has lost its former depth.

Amazement, particularly in old age, is anything but superficial—when we're awake to it. The trouble is, when we *are* much older, we can also gradually lose touch with the richness of our own layers of memory. We slide into a kind of world-weariness or simply get dim, not noticing the world the way we once did. An amazing moment, which often appears with little noise or drama, can be easily missed.

For instance. On a recent morning at the very end of winter, Tom and I were riding in our car just after sunup on our way to the island gym. Cocooned in the warm car by each other's company, we were intent on the plan we'd set for regular walks at the gym, congratulating ourselves for making that happen one more day. We were equally focused on getting back home to a fire in the woodstove and a cup of coffee. All things considered, barely awake, we verged on dim.

A field we drive by all the time then appeared. And through the early morning mist we saw some deer grazing in the low, scant vegetation next to the stone wall along the road. The sight itself wasn't odd. We've encountered plenty of deer throughout our lives, and we often see them on the island. Which means our layers of memory are full of their figures, usually one or two pairs of tawny flanks sprinting for cover.

This was different. It was a posse. We counted eight deer, standing close to where we would pass by. Tom slowed the car. Perhaps because there were so many, it felt as though a ring of enchantment had been thrown around them: *eight large creatures* from a realm connected to ours and also completely separate. Tom and I went quiet. As we pulled near, they stopped eating. The whole herd just stood there, staring at us staring at them. We finally started to drive on, yet none of the animals moved. And whatever dimness previously encased us was gone. In its place, riffling up from the layers, was distilled amazement.

In contrast to childhood, adult amazement steals over us when something happens that's *both* old and new, past and present, lost and found—at least to us. To the next guy there may be nothing remarkable about a herd of deer in a field. Deep amazement arises in us when memories from the layers of our own past connect with something unfolding in the present. And though this might seem as though it's happening only *outside* us; it's actually an inside story, triggered by an outside event.

This is all bound up with how we experience time at different ages. In old age, as time hurtles forward, it pulls us along willy-nilly. And we are conscious of that pull while it's happening. Not so for children. Time can stop for them, in part, because they assume it's eternal; they trust in an endless string of tomorrows. As older people, we experience that same string as increasingly frayed. Short. Undependable.

When old age makes time seem ever shorter, it can astonish us just to wake up and discover we're apparently going to live another day. We're going to put on our shoes and socks and rustle up breakfast again. If our luck holds, and spring is coming, we might see another flock of wild geese headed north, or hear the chorus of spring peepers in the pond across the road, trilling into the evening. If we're alive to the grace of it all, we could find our ordinary dimness pierced by a glimpse of the miraculous-in-the-everyday. And by a subsequent flush of gratitude.

Though children do experience the miraculous all the

time, they normally lack adults' capacity for reflection. It doesn't occur to children to become conscious of what they're unconscious of or to convert that consciousness into gratitude. They might notice the geese going over, but until they're older, gratefulness isn't likely to be part of the noticing. Nor would the birds tend to arouse in children anything called amazement—they're just geese, right? I suspect many such sightings, throughout a lifetime, are required to create the poet's resonant layers. Or to produce the catch in the throat I experience every spring and fall when flocks of geese pass over, themselves a plaintive sign of time on the move.

This feeling of layered experience was very much in play when our young grandchildren would coax us to a beach to participate in their ongoing search for sea glass. That search was especially evocative for me, having memories of identical quests during long-gone summers on these same beaches. I was flat out amazed to sit and watch the children roam up and down the water's edge, backs bent, oblivious to everything but the sandy world at their feet, as I had once been.

Occasionally one of the children would race up the beach to wherever we adults were sitting, to show us a choice for their collections. One glance at their faces told the story: written there was the unmistakable, whole-face takeover induced by a mixture of hope and excitement.

Our job, like my friend's mother long ago, in explaining pearls in mussels, was to handle those faces with kid gloves.

When the children first began to collect the glass, their eyes would cloud over if we had to tell them an entry didn't pass muster – the piece being too recently broken, and therefore too sharp to keep. But. They soon became expert at sighting samples tumbled by tide and time long enough to form the smooth, milky surfaces coveted by all beach glass hunters who know their business. Bringing those mellowed candidates, they gazed at us for a nano-second, earnestly seeking approval. Then, their own time being unlimited, and having not a second of it to waste, they would turn on their heels and dash back to their labors. So are the intricate layers of our own future amazement formed, even if we have no awareness of the process for years to come.

Why does this matter? One big reason: losing the capacity to be amazed can cause life to take on a gloomy cast. It may also render a sense of gratitude hard to find.

Amazement is a pipeline to gratitude—which is, in turn, perhaps our most important possession as older people. By the time we are old, we are richest and strongest if we have a large reservoir of gratitude for all that has befallen us, even the hard events. It's a spiritual issue. Without gratitude, we are spiritually bereft. And gratitude can elude us if we are rarely amazed.

Adults usually want both these qualities to develop in their children and grandchildren. And that happens most naturally through the good fortune of being present when children have their own enchanted experiences, maybe helped along by an adult hand. Children always *hope* to be amazed, even though they often can't believe they actually will be.

Many years ago, Tom and I were spending Christmas with a four-year old grandchild and her family. She was transfixed that year by the image of Santa coming in the night with his team of jingling reindeer, by the unlikely prospect of him touching down at *her* house, bringing presents from the list she had painstakingly written and mailed, and then continuing on his sleigh to children around the world. She simply couldn't believe it might happen. And, of course, she hoped like mad that it would. Just before she and her Christmas-confused baby brother went to bed on Christmas Eve, Tom and I took her outside to scatter the "Reindeer Food with Sparkle" we'd purchased for this moment. It made glittering streaks of promise across the snow, ratcheting up her delighted laugh with every handful tossed. After she finally managed to go to bed, Tom and I went back outside to create our version of hoof marks, messing up the snow in time-honored reindeer fashion, before falling into bed ourselves.

We had been planning to take her out the following morning to show her evidence of the visitation, but she beat us to the punch. She went outside on her own, much earlier in the morning than the world wanted to know about, and then crept into our room with her barely contained whisper... *"Nana...Grampy...the reindeer CAME!"*

You bet they came.

And weren't they amazing.

Dancing to the End

An experience of irrepressible life force can thrill us. And, in the same instant, it can confuse us. We want to lower the intensity, but we also hanker for it to increase, to deliver more of itself, to go on without letup. In the meantime, our tears will often settle the matter.

I remember an evening when I watched a great-niece perform in a summer musical on the island, *becoming* essence of life force in the process. She was about six. She danced and sang her heart out so hard, so winningly, that when the final applause thundered through the room, I understood why an old man sitting next to me turned and, with tears in his eyes, exclaimed, "Who IS that child?" as though he had to know, that very instant, the name of a little girl who could embody so much unbridled vitality. Her name only mattered tangentially, however; the answer to his question was in the tears sliding down his face.

Those tears in an older person are complicated. When we're old, we know what a struggle it can be to maintain our vitality. Plenty conspires against it. Our own life force has normally been bruised enough by the slings and arrows we've endured that our verve is substantially decreased. And yet, whether we're old or not, most of us yearn for the intense moment to come around again, like an emotional brass ring.

In a seemingly unrelated vein, I think of my own mother and the life force she must have had to summon when she found herself pregnant with me. About two years before I came along, she had given birth to full-term twin boys who died at birth, "blue babies" as they were called in those days, dead by any other name. She would never talk about it, but from the pain I saw cross her face the couple of times I raised the subject, the monumental heartache this loss had caused was obvious. Instead of being undone, though, by depression, discouragement, and crippling fear at the possibility of the nightmare reoccurring, she went for it again, with me. And then, maybe less consequentially—maybe—she plowed forward and had both my sisters. In a real sense, although profoundly different from a six-year old spinning across a stage for all she's worth, this is the exact same press of life that made the onlooking old man cry.

Many years ago, I encountered another old man who showed me vitality rekindled, and the close tie between exuberance and tears. I was then a first-semester seminarian in my early forties, doing an internship at a parish church. Michael, the rector of the church and my new boss, asked if I'd like to join him on a pastoral call to this man—

a former parishioner, now in a nursing home, an ancient Welshman named Hugh. I jumped at the chance. As a total pastoral greenhorn, I was eager for close-up experiences of a minister's work. Michael assembled bread and wine for Communion, grabbed a couple of hymnals, and we took off in his car under the pelting rain of a dark November afternoon.

On the drive to the nursing home, I heard pieces of Hugh's story. He was part of the massive river of Europeans who immigrated to the United States after World War I. During the war, he had been with British forces on a brutal tour of duty in the Middle East. That brutality was the chief reason Hugh loved to tell of the brief Christmas truce he participated in when German and British soldiers famously exchanged candy and sang carols together. To Michael, Hugh's radiant recounting of the truce epitomized his enduring vitality, despite his age and all the hardships that had befallen him throughout his life. Those hardships now included being widowed and never having had any children.

As we passed into the interior of the nursing home, I flinched at the smell, hoping my flinch didn't show. There was nothing unusual; it was standard-issue nursing home. But I hadn't been inside one for a long time, and I'd never visited as part of a caregiving team.

We walked onto a corridor with wheelchairs lining one wall, a queue I soon realized pointed the route to Hugh's room. As Michael greeted people in the wheelchairs I followed and tried to imitate him, but I was all thumbs and dry mouth. Most heads lolled; Michael was undeterred. He made his way slowly along the line, taking a moment to acknowledge each person with a smile or a squeeze of the hand. If he knew a name, he spoke it; he never called anybody Dear. In each encounter it seemed he was addressing himself directly to a spirit that might be feeble but hadn't vanished. Crucial lesson learned: we're alive until we're not, and those who may wonder whether they've already died might appreciate a warm word to the contrary.

At one point, I heard a plaintive, eager voice call, "Is that my minister coming, is that my minister?" To which Michael called back, "We're almost there, Hugh!" This rendezvous with the wheelchairs had obviously happened before, to Hugh's cocked ears. And then we were in his room. An epic smile split the worn Welsh face, shriveled arms reached forward from a grimy tee shirt, meeting an immediate bear hug from Michael. Hugh was almost blind, but that didn't prevent him from finding my hand when Michael introduced us. He patted the bed, inviting me to sit down—right close by.

Hugh's connection with Michael soon became clear. The toothless face, now turned from grey to flushed, said it all. *Life itself had come through the door.* Hugh spent most of his days alone with the pale glow of a television set. But now light, real light, had painted the faded room. It was as if the ions in the air reorganized themselves to give him the only news that counted: he was remembered, he was cared for, and younger arms were here again to embrace his thin shoulders with love and energizing courage.

I know now that when Hugh called out, "Is that my minister coming?" it wasn't a request for information. It rose up and over the rim of a deep well of needing to know, once again, that the vital energy arriving today might also, in some form, be in his future. All the way to the end. Hugh gave hints he was aware the respite on this afternoon would be brief, but it wasn't the point. The liveliness we brought was more precious to him than a pot of gold, and he was going to revel in it for however long the visit lasted.

Which is exactly what happened during the next hour, as Hugh hurled himself into a short but intense experience of love on the loose. We bent some nursing home rules, especially those about noise, closing the door and singing hymns at the top of our lungs, a counterpart to the storm raging outside. Hugh knew by heart the Welsh tunes in the Episcopal hymnals we had brought along, and he exhorted us to sing some of them twice. During a lull, Michael encouraged him to recite the Lord's Prayer for me in Welsh, which he did, leaning into the musical language of his childhood with rapturous enthusiasm. And as I urged him on, he recited it again—through the tears in his throat.

Finally, we smoothed the bed and laid the elements for Communion out on top of the bedspread that had seemed so forlorn at first but no longer did. Michael led us in some prayers; we each took bread and wine, with Hugh gulping everything down as though he hadn't eaten for days. When we finished, the three of us held hands for a few quiet moments, drawn together by Communion's profoundly affectionate mystery—a mystery renowned as being wide and deep enough to embrace all comers. That stormy afternoon, we comers were the standard motley bunch: a skillful priest with his own heartaches; an old soldier soon to ride into the setting sun; and a grateful beginner, now just a little more seasoned.

I didn't understand it back then, but over time I realized that if Michael and I sowed courage in Hugh that day, we reaped it from him triple fold. And as Hugh's own vitality shone out, rippling so sweet and strong among the three of us, I absorbed an indelible truth: the life force in us doesn't quit. Too often we assume that signs of its weakening mean it's gone, or will be the closer someone gets to the end. It can become so buried under emotional debris that we think it's finished. But it almost never is. The life force in us each isn't a substance that runs out. It's more like the press of the tide: dependable, oncoming, inexhaustible. And when we encourage the quickening of this force in others, it not only is life-giving for them but gives us courage as well, perhaps inspiring us to dance to the end ourselves.

This was shown to me again at a wedding Tom and I attended not long ago. The occasion itself generated plenty of exuberance: it was a service for two women together for many years and now able to tie a legal knot. The church buzz was already thick, in other words, when the service music began to tune up.

As we stood to the music with everyone else and faced toward the back of the church, Tom and I were startled with pleasure to see his elderly Aunt Frances at the head of the aisle. She was a grandmother to one of the brides, but it hadn't occurred to us she might be part of the ceremony. Though she was a very game woman at ninety-three, she also suffered the usual multiple infirmities of old age. None of those were in evidence that afternoon. Instead, we saw that she was dressed to the nines, had her walker ready to roll, and was sporting a grin as big as her native State of Maine.

Then, as the first chords of "Here Come the Brides" were struck and strengthened, on came Frances, wizened but unbowed, flinging rose petals from a little basket tied to the walker. She took her dignified time, this flower girl plucked from eternity, neither slowing nor hurrying as she made her way toward the front of the church, fully inhabiting the moment. The congregation held its collective breath—not because we worried that she wouldn't complete the trip but because we knew she would. When she reached the end of the aisle, she scattered her last blossoms and backed into the pew, to let the brides glide into place. The two women caused only a slight stir, however, on their arrival. Frances had already brought down the house with applause, raising a rainbow of tears in every eye.

A perceptive observer once advised paying close attention

to our tears, especially when they erupt without warning, usually in a moment of great poignancy. Those tears can ambush people of any age, but are particularly likely to come to those who are older and have spent many decades creating the soul-stirring depths where poignancy hides.

We don't choose our poignant occasions; they come unbidden, piercing in their clarity, often reminding us of something we've forgotten. But those moments may also release a certain piece of our own life force. When a wasted, lonely warrior in a nursing home can summon the pluck to sing his head off; or a mother heartbroken by loss in childbirth can try again; or a withered old woman so close to her own death can steer her walker down a church aisle tossing flowers with abandon, perhaps we can find in them a bit of the bravery needed to dance until the last note ourselves. That is, after all, one of the things we might give each other on the road to the end: a piece of heart, a dose of courage, a spirited wave of the hand.

Postscript

It took us a few more false starts. And feeble attempts. Finally, though, our obituaries are written, funeral services planned, hymns chosen. We've contacted the director of the funeral home to learn the procedure before one of us gets clobbered with the need for it. And to plan for the fees.

We took some cuttings from the rosy-lavender coverlet of wild phlox that nature flings across the island cemetery each May; those transplants will now spread over our plot too. We've chosen a gravestone. Before winter comes again, it will be upright with our names and birth dates, the curves of plain grey stone much to our liking. Later on, the monument company will complete the engraving. The Burning Bush we planted next to where the stone will stand is just a bunch of unpromising sticks right now; in future Octobers it will be a tall shrub, leaves blazing crimson.

When one of us is gone, the other will bring geraniums on Memorial Day, as many people on the island do, and continue to tend the gravesite into the cooler months. If I'm the one doing the tending, I suspect I'll remember the glad afternoon so long ago when we rolled around the cemetery in Vermont, laughing and conjuring babies. Little did either of us understand then that the family we'd end up with would mount a complete takeover of our hearts, needing no further additions from us.

The earthly sorrows and joys Tom and I have shared find their full meaning in this burying place. And that meaning will, as it's supposed to, get diluted here by seasons passing one into the next. Similarly, the space we've occupied in the spirits of those we love and leave will quietly grow smaller, assimilated by time into their new lives, new loves, new hopes. If all goes right, though, the sturdy little phlox will keep rippling rose and lavender over this ground, year after year, under the warm winds of early summer.

Acknowledgments

Enormous thanks to:

Kate Kennedy, wonderful friend and consummate editor.

Ariette Scott, whose enthusiasm and technical wizardry have been indispensable to the creation of this book.

A host of readers offering crucial criticisms and support from the start.

My daughters-by-marriage, Tracy Callahan and Robin Cushman, for strong encouragement of this book and for their steadfast love.

And my husband, Tom, for his deep encouragement of these essays, his editing help, and his loving companionship in everything—large and small.

About the Author

After graduating from the University of Maine, Mary worked as a community organizer, co-owned a vocational rehabilitation firm, and was co-founder and director of the first battered women's shelter in Maine. She also was a principal organizer for the Maine Nuclear Freeze Campaign. In the late 1980's, she and her husband, Tom, graduated from Yale Divinity School, and were ordained as Episcopal priests. They worked in large, urban parishes for a decade, and then established a counseling and spiritual direction practice in Portland, Maine, running it for almost 20 years. They live year-round on nearby Chebeague Island.

Mary is the author of *Strenuous Blessings*, another collection of essays. The Cushmans also wrote *Riding the Passionate Edge*, a book on strengthening relationships.